HONOR HELD DEAR

My View from the Bridge Wing

HONOR HELD DEAR

My View from the Bridge Wing

A reflection on life, perspective, and leadership

Captain Alan E. Eschbach, USN (Ret.)

Edited by Tamurlaine Melby

Brandylane Publishers, Inc.
Publishing books since 1985

Copyright 2017, 2019 by Alan E. Eschbach, USN (Ret.). No part of this book may be reproduced in any form or by any electronic or mechanical means, or the facilitation thereof, including information storage and retrieval systems, without permission in writing from the publisher, except in the case of brief quotations published in articles and reviews. Any educational institution wishing to photocopy part or all of the work for classroom use, or individual researchers who would like to obtain permission to reprint the work for educational purposes, should contact the publisher.

ISBN 978-1-947860-66-7

Library of Congress Control Number: 2017941971

Printed in the United States of America

Published by Brandylane Publishers, Inc.
5 S. 1st Street
Richmond, Virginia 23219
brandylanepublishers.com | belleislebooks.com

Praise for *Honor Held Dear*

"Captain Alan Eschbach has written an honest, moving, and entirely human memoir of his successful voyage in life from SEAL training to command of a Navy destroyer. His lessons "from the bridge wing" reflect his hard-won principles and beliefs and are of great value to any leader."

—Admiral James Stavridis, USN (Ret), Supreme Allied Commander at NATO 2009-2013 and Dean of The Fletcher School of Law and Diplomacy at Tufts University

"The reader of Capt. Eschbach's eloquent memoir will be struck by two things: his courage in the face of adversity and his timeless lessons for leadership and love. *Honor Held Dear* offers the brutally honest perspective of a man who has known both failure and success … and rose above them both. No leader—indeed, no one wishing to lead—can afford to ignore this book."

—Rear Admiral John F. Kirby, USN (Ret), Assistant Secretary of State for Public Affairs (2015-2017)

"Captain Eschbach and his book are a testament that humility, integrity, and leading by example are the hallmarks of good leadership, and that respect and loyalty are best earned through these leadership traits. The lessons in life found within the pages of *Honor Held Dear* are a must read for one of any age and station in life."

—Delegate James A. "Jay" Leftwich, Virginia General Assembly, 78th House District and Managing Partner, Basnight, Kinser, Leftwich & Nuckolls, PC

"The powerful emotional rollercoaster that is *Honor Held Dear* continuously brings the reader pride, laughter, and tears. Captain Alan Eschbach was a different kind of leader; one that naturally inspired his sailors to perform at their utmost. To them, he was one of their own. His crew didn't feel they had to follow, they wanted to, and expecting their best, he got their best. If one were asked to serve under Alan Eschbach's leadership again, I would be first in line."

—Fire Controlman Second Class (SW)(SAR) Brady N. Alland, USN and Hollywood actor, writer, and director

Life every man holds dear; but the dear man holds honor far more precious dear than life.

—William Shakespeare

Contents

Author's Note—*The Bridge Wing* xi
Preface xiii

Part I: The Influences of My Youth

    Chapter One—Lancaster County, Pennsylvania 1

    Chapter Two—My Parents 18

    Chapter Three—My Brother 36

    Chapter Four—Grampa 43

    Chapter Five—Coach Harrington 55

    Chapter Six—My First True Hero 60

Part II: Life beyond the Southern End

    Chapter Seven—Millersville State College 64

    Chapter Eight—Getting "Hammered" in Newport 72

    Chapter Nine—USS *Pharris* 76

    Chapter Ten—BUD/S 84

    Chapter Eleven—Hell Week 98

Part III: The Road from BUD/S to Command at Sea

    Chapter Twelve—USS *Thomas S. Gates* 126

    Chapter Thirteen—The Naval Command and Staff College . . 142

    Chapter Fourteen—USS *John S. McCain* 145

    Chapter Fifteen—The Pentagon 152

    Chapter Sixteen—Naval Surface Force, Atlantic 157

Part IV: USS *Arleigh Burke*

Chapter Seventeen—Turning Over with a Good Friend 162

Chapter Eighteen—My First Challenge 165

Chapter Nineteen—Forming New Bonds 168

Chapter Twenty—Pre-deployment Workups 170

Chapter Twenty-One—Deployment 179

Chapter Twenty-Two—My Best Day 185

Part V: My View from the Bridge Wing

Chapter Twenty-Three—Duty and Personal Responsibility . . 192

Chapter Twenty-Four—Leadership Styles 212

Chapter Twenty-Five—Athletics and Leadership 218

Chapter Twenty-Six—When Expected to Lead — Lead 223

Chapter Twenty-Seven—The Slippery Slope 228

Chapter Twenty-Eight—Common Courtesy 231

Chapter Twenty-Nine—Service and Support 235

Chapter Thirty—What Time Revealed to Me 241

Epilogue—*My Journal* 243

Acknowledgements 245

About the Author 247

AUTHOR'S NOTE

THE BRIDGE WING

For those who go to sea on ships, the bridge wing represents much more than simply a physical extension of the pilot house. During risky ship maneuvering situations, the bridge wing is where you'll find the captain, for the captain is the one ultimately and irrevocably responsible for the safe maneuvering of the ship. Someone else may be giving orders to the helm, but the captain always maintains the mantle of command.

While the bridge wing's designed purpose is to allow for an unobstructed vantage point from which to direct and observe the ship's movement, its intangible value lies in what it represents to the captain. Given the enormity of the responsibilities inherent in command at sea, as well as the physical and mental fatigue associated with always being on watch, there is an unbreakable bond between a captain and his ship and crew, allowing only rare opportunities for solitude or reflection.

On those rare occasions at sea when the captain finds an opportunity for introspection, you'll find him on the bridge wing, his personal oasis. For a ship's captain, the bridge wing represents the part of his life where his years of experience are needed the most. It is the bridge wing where decisions determining the ship's success or failure are often made within the passing of a single heartbeat or breath. As captain of USS *Arleigh Burke* and USS *San Jacinto*, the bridge wing was my haven for reflection. It was my place to regain a lost perspective, and the place I often found perfect clarity in my thoughts. Decisions I had made were frequently affirmed and sometimes softened there.

For most professional mariners whose sailing days are "past and opening," the bridge wing is the place most missed and most fondly remembered. I would imagine nearly all professions have a comparable aspect that is missed in similar ways by those who move on or retire. A farmer's bridge wing might be the seat of a tractor while plowing, planting, or harvesting a remote field. For others, it might be found during the solitude of a run, in a family kitchen or backyard. Wherever it is, the bridge wing is that place where the challenges of life seem to untangle and align more smoothly. It is where we make sense of this life and discover what's truly in our hearts.

Preface

Growing up in a small Pennsylvania Dutch farming community, I never dreamed of commanding a ship at sea. In fact, I don't recall having any dreams. Even though from a young age I knew I'd join the navy after high school, I didn't give a second thought to what might lie beyond my initial tour. Back then my horizons, and certainly my interests, extended no farther than the next trout stream, field, or forest that surrounded my home in southern Lancaster County. I simply wanted the "challenge of the sea" to test my manhood, as it has for generations of other young men. I had no fancier motive than that it seemed like another good adventure.

Yet each year, hundreds of incoming freshmen (plebes, rats, swabs, or knobs) attending the service academies or other commissioning sources miss that sense of simply competing against life's challenges. Rather, they skip to the end, beginning their careers with grand dreams of eventually becoming admirals leading fleets, or generals commanding divisions of men. Their decisions, calculated and tailored every step of their careers, prevent meaningful impact and change. Such lofty aspirations and the tempering of decisions never factored into my vision of the path I'd chosen.

The reality is that for every one hundred prospective officers, only a select few ever reach the highest levels of command—the odds of doing so are similar to the odds of reaching the pinnacle in any profession, whether you work for a Fortune 500 company or play a sport professionally. For every child who achieved their dream of flying into outer space, there were tens of thousands sharing that same dream who fell short of realizing it. Yet that act of "falling short" can often influence, and even define, a life in adverse ways. As a naval officer I knew numerous men who, failing to achieve their dream of command-at-sea, felt disgraced by that failure—burdened by the weight of unfulfilled aspirations, a weight that ultimately affected the rest of their professional careers, and even overshadowed their worth as parents, spouses, or simply citizens.

Witnessing this, I became resolved to stay true to myself and the manner of how I led my life rather than where my career took me. While I am grateful beyond words for having had the opportunity to serve in command of a ship, I still wonder whether realizing that milestone defined the quality of my success and time in the navy.

What I do know is that following my own code did not lead to calmer seas. Following the code meant walking the walk, standing my ground against abusive and degrading practices, and confronting wrong where I saw it. And while the navy is built upon proud legacy and tradition, there are destructive customs and behaviors among sailors, both officers and enlisted, that have crept into our navy culture. Over the course of my career, I repeatedly encountered institutionalized and accepted behaviors at odds with my convictions about how leaders should conduct themselves, and how they should treat those with whom they serve. Thus, at each rung of the ladder leading to command of a ship, I was challenged not only to perform my best as a naval officer, but to attempt to reshape the mindsets of my fellow shipmates in order to form better teams and foster a better culture. It was possibly a quixotic ideal, but I gave it my best shot.

As I reflected back on the decisions and choices I made in my life and career, it became apparent that my upbringing in the Pennsylvania Dutch countryside was crucial to forging my character, conduct, and the manner in which I've approached life's crossroads. This book is a reflection on that journey from the heart of the Pennsylvania Dutch countryside to command of USS *Arleigh Burke*. But more importantly, it is my attempt to continue changing mindsets now that my time as a naval officer has ended. It is my belief that, like life, leading is all about the journey. That it's not the "ends" that matter; rather, it's the manner in which the path is walked.

Part One
The Influences of My Youth

When I hear someone sigh, "Life is hard," I am always tempted to ask, "Compared to what?"

– *Sydney J. Harris*

Part One

The Innocence of My Youth

CHAPTER ONE

LANCASTER COUNTY, PENNSYLVANIA

On the morning of March 3, 2001, I sat aboard USS *Arleigh Burke*, minutes from relinquishing the most rewarding job of my life: captaincy of the first and finest guided missile Aegis destroyer in the United States Navy.

I was grateful beyond words for the chance to command at sea. It had been the experience of a lifetime; but more importantly, it had been a role that validated my life's beliefs—beliefs that went against the grain of not only traditional naval officer thinking, but the thinking of many men in our (American) culture. Among these beliefs was my conviction that naval customs and the behavior of men can be changed for the better, and in doing so, the well being of an entire crew improved.

From the day I arrived aboard my first ship, USS *Pharris*, I had felt more than a little out of place among the other officers. This was no reflection on the fine officers, crews, or commanding officers I had the privilege of working for. Rather, it was my own gut sense that certain navy traditions were fostering a climate that denigrated its people rather than motivating them—traditions that isolated groups within the broader scope of men, making the creation of a truly cohesive team almost unachievable. And so evolved my own quiet quest to *change* things for the better as I navigated through my career—one assignment at a time.

Yet now, as I neared the end of my command tour, having run the gauntlet, I sat under the Arabian Gulf March sky on *Arleigh Burke*, plagued with doubts and overwhelmed by a sea of emotion. It felt as if I were losing my wife and kids to another man. I felt guilt for those moments when I hadn't appreciated the privilege of command and the people as much as I should have, even if those moments had only been fleeting and infrequent. I thought about the times I had been especially demanding of my officers, about my expectations that they show compassion for their people, and about my intolerance of anything I perceived as a lack of personal code, toughness, or physical endurance equal to the demands of the job. I felt humility for how much the crew had done to support and accept me, and I felt even greater humility and pride for having been given the privilege of commanding the lead ship of the class named in honor of Admiral Arleigh A. Burke, a man who had given so much to our navy.

In the weeks leading up to this day, I often found my mind wandering back to my youth as I reflected on how my life's decisions carried me from the village of Rawlinsville, Pennsylvania, to the deck of a guided missile destroyer in Manama, Bahrain. Very often throughout my career, and especially during my tour aboard *Arleigh Burke*, I relied greatly on the experiences and perspective I developed growing up in that small farming community in the heart of the Pennsylvania Dutch. And now, in my final hours aboard ship, and as my strike group commander spoke, I drifted back for one more visit to the place and the people that shaped me . . .

∽

It was a hot, muggy day in August 1967. I was nine years old, and my mother and I were shopping at the general store in Quarryville,

Pennsylvania, buying new clothes for the upcoming school year. This was a yearly ritual that signaled the end of summer was right around the corner.

For most in that area, clothes were bought only when absolutely necessary. Pants too short or shirts with torn sleeves were not reasons enough to buy replacements. Hand-me-downs were a part of life, and I recall proudly wearing the clothes previously worn by sons of my parents' good friends, clothes that had likely been owned by others before them.

As my mother and I idled under the store's lone ceiling fan, and she held pants to my small frame to observe how much growth they'd allow, my gaze was drawn to a man standing next to a rack of overalls. Beside him was a woman who I assumed was his wife, flipping through the display. I'm not certain what it was about him that held my attention, but I could sense something *different*.

Like many men in southern Lancaster County, he was certainly a farmer. Farmers bore that universal look: faded denim coveralls, John Deere ball caps, and skin on their faces and necks that was sun-browned and weathered in deep creases and seams. Farmers rarely looked around when they came to town, instead walking with a purposeful forward lean—not in a rush, but at a steady work-all-day pace—knowing precisely what they intended to buy before entering any store. Farmers in my hometown didn't *shop*, and if they had questions about an item or machinery part, they always asked in a direct but respectful manner.

On the occasion when a farmer *did* go shopping, having been successfully trapped by his wife, it was an ordeal. Then he became as intractable as a dog being dragged to the vet, reluctantly following her, tugging on his collar, fidgeting, his mind wandering back to that broken hydraulic line on the tractor that needed fixing, or that bent steel rake long overdue for welding.

This farmer's discomfiture was different, though. He didn't fidget a bit, standing painfully still in a guarded fashion, like a man who'd been sentenced. There was a pinch of suffering in his eyes, tempered by an intense resolve.

As if sensing I was staring at him, he suddenly turned toward me. It was then that I noticed the way one side of his shirt appeared much bigger than the other and seemed to hang off his shoulder. Yet I still wasn't sure what I was seeing when I felt the abrupt grip of my mother's hand on my shoulder as she spun me forcefully back toward her. In that instant, I realized what had been holding my attention: the man's right arm was missing.

Almost immediately I began shifting my eyes sheepishly back in his direction, both to better see the extent of his loss and to ensure he hadn't seen me staring. But as my gaze reached his face, I was horrified to see his eyes fixed on mine.

He wasn't angry, though he had every reason to be—both with me for staring and with the accident that took his arm. Instead he gave me a grin that was reassuring, even apologetic, as if to cushion the horror he knew I was feeling. His eyes relaxed from their pinched focus into a fatherly understanding, freeing me from my shock and embarrassment. He had no doubt seen that look on the faces of other children, and come to a place from which he was able to offer comfort rather than contempt. Like others in Lancaster County maimed by life, this man had taken what life handed him and resolutely continued onward.

Of all the things I experienced as a young boy, this brief interaction, more than any other, would shape how I dealt with challenges later in life. Going forward, I would always compare my place in the world to that farmer's.

After that encounter, I never again felt entitled to anything, feeling it selfish to ask my parents or anyone else for anything. A day of work was simply a day of work. It didn't need categorizing as easy or hard. The only relevant thing was how I tackled that day's work—not how, or even *if*, I got paid. Although I certainly had preferences, I never felt that I deserved or needed more than I had. I would come to learn that feeling was common in Lancaster County.

∽

Pennsylvania has a rich heritage. For centuries, it was highly prized by Native American tribes who fought desperately for control of the lowlands, its streams, and the abundance of game. Its rivers and land are still defined by their tribal names: the Lenape (later known as the Delaware), the Niagara and Wyoming, the fierce and powerful Seneca, the Poconos, and the Susquehannocks.

The last tribe standing was the Susquehannocks. Weakened by relentless attacks from the Seneca to the north and Delaware to the east, the proud Susquehannocks were eventually driven out or enslaved. European incursion and smallpox further laid waste to the tribal remnants. The last of the tribe members were massacred by southern Pennsylvania vigilantes known as the "Paxton boys." Benjamin Franklin raised a militia in an attempt to protect the Susquehannock survivors from the ruthless Paxtons but failed. And so faded the Native American nations from southeastern Pennsylvania, leaving behind only their legacy namesakes.

Fittingly, though, it was the Amish (a Quaker sect) who inherited claim to the Lancaster region. These non-violent Europeans would prove to be fine stewards of the land and have shaped its character for three hundred years.

Anyone visiting Lancaster County can immediately sense it's a place out of time, like Brigadoon. There are horse-drawn wagons and Amish buggies on the roads, and young Amish boys working alongside sturdy bearded men in the fields. Living without electricity or modern conveniences, the Amish are dependent upon the work of their hands. Moreover, that German instinct for hard work and self-reliance is not unique to the Amish, but is a constant throughout the region I still call home. The inhabitants of Lancaster County march to a seasonal clock, tied to the land through shared values of human decency, self-reliance, and communal effort.

Farming, trout fishing, trapping, hunting, and athletics dominate the daily rhythms of life in Lancaster County. And while baseball and football are popular, wrestling really rules. Wrestlers value personal strength and self-sufficiency, traits that characterize most men and women in the region. Wrestling is *the* sport that all boys possessing an athletic spirit begin in the first grade and stay with until they can no longer make the team. (For me, that time came in the tenth grade.)

But while farming and sports are fixations throughout the year, nothing—and I mean nothing—dominates the fall like hunting in Lancaster County, particularly for the men. Hunting is the tradition that bonds father and son, and the woods and fields are where life's lessons are learned and reinforced season after season, sometimes being the only common ground besides blood to unite generations of family members. Even today in Lancaster County, hunting brings forth a legacy unchanged since the days of tribes, frontiersmen, and settlers.

The start of hunting season represents a fixed point on the seasonal clock that every Lancaster County resident anticipates. Even those no longer able to hunt still cast a watchful eye to the countryside in the hopes they'll see something significant to share with those who will soon head to the woods. Come September, rifles and bows are taken out of gun cabinets or off walls in nearly every household to be lovingly tuned and prepped for the season. An unofficial holiday exists in rural Pennsylvania to accommodate for the inevitable absence of so many boys and girls from school on the opening day of deer season. Conversations in feed stores and schools shift to weather, the best caliber of guns, tales of past hunts, and recent sightings of the buck of a lifetime.

Given the rhythm of life there, events taking place outside of Pennsylvania have little reach into Lancaster County. It's not that inhabitants don't care, but when working tirelessly from sunrise to sunset, one's perspective is front-sight focused. In the mid-1960s (the decade when I attended grade school), Vietnam, China's cultural revolution, Angola, and Soviet overtures to Cuba came to my hometown as distant echoes from far-off places, barely real.

To my knowledge, there were never any anti-war demonstrations in Lancaster. Most boys who got drafted simply did their hitch, and then returned to their farms and fields, keeping the brutality and inhumanity of combat securely within the confines of their minds. Those who died in the war returned as well, to be mourned, honored, and buried. Regardless of religion, these men became united with the legacy of those who passed before them: Dutch and English settlers, Lenape, Seneca, and Susquehannock tribal peoples, and American servicemen from every conflict since. All taken, Lancaster County's inhabitants are stoically inclined, at home with self-denial and sacrifice.

∽

Within the "Southern End" of Lancaster County, my roots are more specifically planted in the village of Rawlinsville, a town so small, it's more like an intersection with a stop sign. Rawlinsville is located about fifteen miles south of the city of Lancaster, completely surrounded by the rolling hills, pastures, woods, and farms that make up most of the county's fertile soil. Although my mother grew to love Rawlinsville, she would later confess that when she first moved there from Boston, it struck her as remote and untamed. To Mom, Rawlinsville was completely untouched by time and technology, and was the last place on earth she wanted to be. My view couldn't have been more different.

As a kid, I could hardly have asked for more adventurous or rustic surroundings. I could step out my back door and walk through nothing but fields and woods for the entire day, something my brother and I did often while growing up. Before I was old enough to hunt, I would spend my fall Saturdays perched in the kitchen window with my shotgun, watching our backyard for hours, waiting for a pheasant to venture within range. The rest of the day would seem like weeks as I waited for my dad to return home from hunting so I could show him my kill, feeling pleased that I was already becoming a good hunter.

My life in the Southern End, as it was called, was absolutely wonderful. One-room schoolhouses dotted the countryside, and horse-drawn plows were a more common sight in the fields than gas-powered farm equipment. Every store and merchant shop had hitching posts for the Amish to tie up their horses, and they still do today. The Amish were an integral part of the community, and there was never any undue local interest in their lives. In fact, the cultural differences that were so glaring and obvious to tourists felt completely irrelevant—if not invisible—to those who lived in their midst.

When viewed from a car window, life in Lancaster County appears picturesque and idyllic, almost "Shire-like." It's a world utterly at odds with reality. The orderly countryside and scenic farms come at the high cost of immense labor and human risk. In the 1960s, there were more than thirty thousand farms in eastern Pennsylvania. The U.S. Department of Agriculture reported that farming-related accidents occurred daily, with agriculture workers facing a one-in-thirty chance of severe injury and a one-in-seventy chance of death. It was a daily lottery with no minimum age requirement and ever-increasing odds of "winning." For a man who farmed for twenty years, his chances of a limb getting maimed by drive belts, spinning gears, or cutting blades rose to a staggering 50 percent, with his risk of death hovering just above 20 percent. Meaning every morning as the farmer grabbed his coffee and headed out to the fields or barn it was a fifty-fifty crapshoot against fate. Is it any wonder farmers carry the same hardened look of strain as those who have been to battle?

In school, I shared classrooms with friends who would be there one day and gone the next, staying home to work the family farm while an injured father recovered. Upon their return to school, they'd receive a pat on the back or an empathetic smile (the only thing you could offer), and then they'd go about struggling to rediscover the sense of humor and unburden they'd once enjoyed. They'd sit in class without expression, and walk to their next class alone and reticent.

Because of those surroundings, for as long as I can remember I have been acutely aware not only of life's blessings, but of how quickly they can evaporate. As a young boy, I recall trout fishing alone and often stopping to gaze around at the beauty of the outdoors, knowing even then that those moments could be fleeting. For reasons that would only be revealed to me with time, I was blessed with that rare sensitivity, and it has allowed me to pause in appreciation of individual moments—and to give thanks for my physical ability to enjoy life fully.

During my teenage years, if I wasn't working, running, hunting, trapping, or fishing, I spent almost every spare moment just exploring the woods. I'd get up long before sunrise, throw on my well-worn hunting pants and my dad's olive drab parka from his time in the navy during the early 1950s, and drive out to Muddy Run Park. The park had been built around a newly formed reservoir near the Susquehanna River and was surrounded by a fence, which allowed the wildlife within its boundary to flourish.

I knew from spending hours inside the park the exact place where I could squeeze through the fence undetected and far away from the main entrance. Entering from this remote part of the park put me into an area that was rarely violated by visitors—right in the thick of the deer's primary habitat.

One morning in 1974, when I was sixteen, I did just that. The weather was perfect: about forty degrees with a heavy drizzle, which allowed me to sneak around in virtual silence. It also served as a deterrent to other park goers. From my many visits, I knew nearly all of the bedding areas for the hundreds of deer that lived inside the fence, and the best vantage points from which to spot them in transit between their feeding areas and beds. And while these deer were as wild and wary as any that lived outside the park, I could distinguish most of them from one another, and could even trace the bucks' bloodlines based on characteristics of their antlers.

This morning, I sat concealed by ground cover until about 10:00 a.m., and then decided to sneak quietly back toward the opening in the fence. My normal practice was to move just ten to fifteen feet at a time and then sit or stand for a few minutes to look for movement. After one such stop, I was getting ready to take my next few steps when I caught movement. I was soon able to make out a deer lying down some 150 yards away.

Determination and perseverance are two qualities that served me well in my military career, and that morning in the woods they merged in a curious way that yielded one of the most wondrous experiences of my young life. Keeping my eyes on the doe I had just spotted, I stood perfectly still until I could tell for sure she was looking in the opposite direction, then slowly worked myself to the ground. For the next two and a half hours I crawled, barely an inch at a time, to see how close I could get to her. I moved with my face to the ground, only occasionally raising it to stay on course, through piles of deer scat and an increasingly heavy rain that soaked through my clothes. Even though I was no fan of frigid weather, I was oblivious to how wet and chilled I had become. I was focused solely on sneaking up on the deer.

After hours in the cold rain, I found myself in the midst of five deer, all bedded down within ten to fifteen yards of one another. I was stunned they hadn't yet sensed me. I had always been told as a child that white-tailed deer have keen senses of sight and smell, yet they were clueless to my presence. The deer closest to me was no more than three feet away by the time I stopped. I could see her body move up and down as she breathed. Every little detail was perfectly clear.

Lying there, I wanted so badly to reach out and touch that doe, but I knew any further movement would likely not have gone unnoticed. After a few more minutes, the effects of the cold and rain began to register, and I felt I'd had enough fun for the morning. So I decided to simply stand and watch them run.

As soon as I rose, the deer exploded to their feet and began dashing back and forth, not knowing which way to run. In the chaos, one of the smaller deer ran right into my chest and knocked me to the ground. I instinctively rolled onto my side to prevent having my groin stepped on, and wrapped my arms around my head to avoid being kicked there as well. When I was confident all the deer had settled on their paths of departure, I stood in amazement and watched them run away.

∽

While my father wasn't a farmer, farming was a way of life that touched everyone in the Southern End. So it was inevitable that my unsupervised explorations would be complemented by that other element of rural living: farm work. For me, this was an experience gained on the farms of friends and neighbors, and I attribute much of my life's work ethic to the time I spent tending land and livestock, for no more reason or compensation than knowing a neighbor needed help and my hands were free to provide it.

It wasn't uncommon for the children in my area to come together to help their friends carry out various seasonal farming rituals that were simply too much work for immediate family to accomplish alone. Thus, from time to time, I would be called upon to help a classmate's father change out the chickens on their farm. As I recall, most of the chicken farmers in the area had between twenty thousand and sixty thousand chickens, and when they were past their egg-laying years, they had to be changed out for a new crop. Over the course of a few days or a week, several friends and I would go to the farm and begin the process of removing the old chickens from their crates, then cleaning and prepping the chicken houses before putting in the new birds.

Although the work was dirty, I loved being with my friends, because interspersed with the work was lots of good-natured trash talking and ribbing. One thing I came to realize over the years was that, for those from my part of Pennsylvania, the next best thing to doing anything was talking about it. So a night at the local chicken farm provided plenty of material for talking and laughing about later at school.

The standard practice for getting the chickens out of their cages and into the waiting trucks was pretty straightforward: each person would reach into a cage with one hand and grab a single leg from three different chickens before pulling them from the cage. Once those three were securely in your grasp, you would repeat the action with your other hand. The next step was to walk out of the chicken house with six chickens trying to fly out of your hands, while an adult or older teenager waited on the flatbed truck to take the chickens from you and transfer them to crates for transportation.

As was the case with every other farm chore I performed, the older kids would provide a quick demonstration of what to do, and then it was up to you to figure out the rest. Any subtleties of technique were to be learned later, the hard way. Thinking back to the anticipatory looks on the older kids' faces, I'm pretty sure some of those omissions were intentional.

On these farms, there was a clear pecking order amongst the kids. The older kids had earned the right to do the easier work, while the younger kids got the harder, dirtier jobs. Much like the naval rite of passage that occurs when old salts send the new guys in search of the "mail buoy" or "relative bearing grease" (neither of which exists), watching newbies perform the dirtiest, toughest chores provided some comic relief for the more seasoned farm boys.

When it came to changing out chickens, the most important thing to learn—which was not part of the initial training session—was that chickens don't go without a struggle. Even after being secured in your hands, they flap their wings violently to get free. As a relatively small ten-year-old, I quickly learned that my "wingspan" was critically smaller than the wingspan of the chickens I was carrying. It wasn't long before a perfectly placed wing slap to my groin knocked me to my knees. The kids on the truck nearly fell off laughing, but somehow I managed to hold all six chickens tightly in my hands, gather myself, and stand back up without dropping a single chicken. I was in a moderate amount of discomfort, but I felt a flush of pleasure: the other kids might be laughing, but we all knew I had passed the test.

At that moment, I couldn't know how many more such rites I would encounter in my life—the challenges of military training and rank dynamics were a long way off—but I learned an important lesson that day that would see me through again and again: approach such trials with equal doses of grit and good humor, and everyone wins.

∽

When I was growing up, my mother made it a priority for our family to eat dinner together. I imagine many families were like mine—eating dinner every night at the same time with everyone in their assigned seats. Mom and Dad sat at either end of the table, my sister, Marion, sat on a bench against the wall, and my younger brother, Eddie, and I sat on the opposite side, with me next to Dad. After dinner Mom and Dad would go into the TV room to watch the news while Marion and I would do the dishes. Eddie would get out of kitchen duty because he was the youngest by three years and would have only been in our way in the small kitchen.

One evening during dinner, when I was in the sixth grade, the phone rang. The call was from a friend of my father's who had four sons, one of whom was a classmate and close friend of mine since kindergarten. The man's oldest son had run away from home, so the farmer was calling in search of another set of hands to help work on his farm. My father listened quietly while his friend said his piece. Then Dad replied, "Al will be there first thing in the morning."

He hung up the phone, sat back down at the table, and told me what he'd just agreed to. Up to that point in my life, my only exposure to farm work (besides changing out the chickens) had been performing small chores while visiting friends who lived on farms. I really knew nothing that I thought would be of value to a farmer. Still, early the next morning my mother drove me to the farm, where I was immediately put to work doing what needed to be done.

Most days were passed in the farmer's acres of tobacco and hay. We spent the next month or so topping and suckering the tobacco, baling hay, and later putting it up in the barn. When we weren't out in the fields, we'd turn our attention to milking the herd of roughly forty Holstein cows or doing other ancillary maintenance-type chores.

Eating meals in the field was something I came to enjoy as much as I had anything in my life up to then. It's difficult to explain exactly how it made me feel—I just knew it felt nice. Perhaps it was because for the first time in my life I felt I'd really earned my meal. Maybe it was because the anticipation of a break from the work provided an indescribable sense of excitement. I do know sitting there with the other boys and their father—all of us dirty and sweaty—gave me my first true glimpse of how teamwork builds camaraderie, and how good that feels.

Midmorning, the farmer's wife would take a break from barn and household chores to drive out in a pickup truck to the field where we worked, bringing apples, watermelon, or cantaloupe, and a big pickle jar of ice water we'd all share. Again that pecking order determined who sat where and who drank first. The oldest brother got to sit on the side or tailgate of the truck, while my friend and I would sit on the farm machinery, a pile of tobacco lath, or the ground as we waited for our turn at the pickle jar. The farmer would stand with his wife, who always wore a light, flowery dress, her hair pulled back in a ponytail, her face glistening with perspiration. They truly seemed to adore and respect one another.

The days on the farm turned into weeks, and by the end of my summer there I had become just like everyone else. I wasn't the little kid who was no value added. I had become a fully incorporated member of the family. My time on the farm reminded me of my dad's description of life at sea, where he said the days would often pass like weeks and the weeks would pass like days. I couldn't wait for Friday evening to roll around, when my mother would come and take me home for the weekend. It wasn't that I didn't enjoy the hard work; it was simply that I missed running wild with Eddie. Sometimes, the stretch from Monday to Friday seemed like one long, busy day.

As I began to feel like one of the boys, I started to clown around with my classmate and his older brothers when the opportunity arose. Life with my dad had taught me you can make a game out of anything, and I especially enjoyed games that involved throwing something or running, strengths I had discovered at a young age. Each day when my friend and I would go to one of the outer pastures, I'd insist we race. I always gave my friend a head start, but on one occasion, he simply took off laughing, saying I couldn't catch him.

His advantage didn't last, and it wasn't long before I had passed him and was zipping along the little dirt road, looking over my shoulder and laughing my butt off. It was an unfamiliar road—leading to a pasture I'd never been to before—which is why I didn't know what dangled in my path. Suddenly, pain slashed across my chest and shoulders as something unseen tore through my white T-shirt and into my flesh.

I came to an abrupt stop and observed what had happened: a single strand of barbed wired that stretched across the road was now stuck in my chest. The barbs had torn through my shirt, which was already spotting red with blood. My friend caught up, laughing at first, but stopping when he saw my chest. Strange as it sounds, my first reaction, after assessing the source of my pain and dealing with the discomfort of pulling my chest and shoulders from the barbs, was to think that I had gotten what I deserved for my daily tormenting of my friend. Had the wire been about six inches higher, the outcome could have been much worse.

When we got back to the barn with the cows, we made up a story about how I had been injured. My friend's mother cleaned out my wounds and gave me one of my friend's T-shirts to wear for the rest of the day. She then hand-washed my shirt and hung it up on the clothesline that stretched from the house to the shed. That shirt, damaged as it was, became my favorite article of clothing to wear from that day until the day my mother finally converted it into a rag.

During our breaks my friend and I would sometimes pull a piece of hay or tall weed from the ground, lay it across an electrified fence, and see how long we could hold on before letting go. Other times we would take his BB gun and shoot frogs down at the pond. He never argued when I insisted on being the one to swim out and get those that were beyond our reach from the bank. Seeing my friend's mother put the plate of baked frog legs on the dinner table made me feel good about being able to provide something for the meal.

For my work that summer I was never paid in money. On some occasions when my mom would come pick me up, the farmer's wife would tell her to open her trunk so she could fill it with freshly picked vegetables as payment for my work. At the end of the summer, after I'd earned the respect of the entire family, my mom picked me up and I went home. I remember the father giving me a firm handshake and a pat on the shoulder with his thanks, while my friend's mother gave me the most sincere hug I had ever received from someone other than my mother.

Of all the events that summer that came to hold meaning for me, the most important occurred after the second week of being on the farm. We had just finished making sure all the rafters in the barn were ready for tobacco when the oldest brother came to me and said that when he heard I would be coming out to help, he didn't think I would be of any use, but that I had proven him wrong. From that experience I had learned so much, and had begun to realize and appreciate the value of hard work and the unique privilege of living in that community. Although at the time I didn't really know how unique living there was or how it was influencing my perspective, what I did begin to realize was that I could do just about anything I put my mind and body into.

Looking back, I realize the Southern End was a community seemingly devoid of arrogance, with little interest or curiosity into what went on beyond the farms and fields. There was no sense that any of us were missing whatever it might be that a city life could provide, and there was no expectation that life would ever owe us something more than what we had. I loved the simplicity of that life and the absolute freedom to do all the things I enjoyed most as a boy.

CHAPTER TWO

My Parents

Like most of us, my earliest influences came from my parents: Joan Batley Colley and Everett Good Eschbach. I couldn't have been luckier than to have them. Mom was the ideal mother—loving, tireless, and most of all, protective. Dad was strong and athletic, and did all those outdoor things that made life exciting for a young boy. While my parents seemed the perfect fit for one another, they couldn't have come from more different upbringings.

Dad was the youngest of five children. His closest sibling in age was my Aunt Betty, who was nearly ten years older. With three older sisters and a doting mother, he was spoiled from the time he was born. His home life was happy, loving, and comfortable, enabling him to spend his youth doing the things he enjoyed most—playing baseball, hunting, and trout fishing. I doubt he ever knew one day without having everything he needed and wanted in life. He had it all.

By every account my father lived a perfectly carefree adolescent life. Recognized as a superb athlete and baseball player, after high school he was invited to pursue a career with the New York Giants. Despite getting off to a great start, an injury abruptly ended that dream during his first spring training. In his final pitching appearance prior to his injury, he pitched four and one-third innings of no-hit baseball against the Brooklyn Dodgers.

To put some distance between himself and those back home who had been following his every move toward the big leagues, Dad enlisted in the navy, where he served aboard USS *Lloyd B. Thomas* (DD 764) for more than four years as a storekeeper. The ship was stationed in New England and it was during one of Dad's train rides back to the ship that he met my mother, who was on her way back to nursing school in Malden, Massachusetts.

In contrast to my dad's stable and loving childhood, Mom's couldn't have been more volatile and uncertain. In 1931, Joan Batley Colley, daughter of Maynard Colley and Marion Batley, was born on the dining room table of a Boston boardinghouse for unwed mothers. Because her mother was barely sixteen at the time and unmarried, she was immediately put into the foster care system, where she remained until taken in by her grandmother at age two.

When her grandmother died in 1939, Mom was only eight and believed that it was actually her mother—not her grandmother—who had died. At that point her mother assumed custody of her, and Mom went to live with her biological father, Maynard, and brother, Eddie, in Portland, Maine.

Growing up, Mom experienced more difficult circumstances than most children. She knew the feelings of being unwanted, and of not knowing where she belonged or how she fit in. She knew the loneliness of being a part of a broken, dysfunctional family, and the confusion and turmoil caused by an abusive alcoholic father.

When the last of her two siblings, Alan Colley, was born, Mom was ten and found her greatest sense of worth in being her two brothers' biggest protector. Mom would shield them as best she could from the abuse of their father and the insensitivity of their mother. She provided for them when her parents either couldn't or wouldn't, and she even stood up for her mother after her father had beaten her so badly it left her mother's ribs and nose broken.

When Mom graduated from high school, she left Maine to attend nursing school in Malden, Massachusetts, where she met my father. After a whirlwind romance, they married only days before Dad's final deployment in the navy. Upon his return home and his honorable discharge, they moved into an apartment owned by Dad's parents in his hometown of Rawlinsville, Pennsylvania. Just as Mom's childhood was vastly different from Dad's, so too was Rawlinsville strikingly different from the city life she had known in Portland, Maine. However, what was consistent was Mom's genuine charm. And she used that charm to begin thawing the stoic demeanors of Dad's family. Her kindness and affection endeared her to them and set the stage for a wonderful relationship.

∞

At the top of the list of the people who have most influenced me is my father. Many of my childhood friends referred to him as the Daniel Boone of Southeastern Pennsylvania and often told me they wished he were their father. Although I loved being with my dad, trying to keep up with him and live up to his reputation was difficult at times.

When my father returned from the navy to Rawlinsville in 1954, his father was able to get him a job as a bank teller for the Bank of Lancaster County in the small town of Quarryville, just six miles east of Rawlinsville. My grandfather thought his son's bookkeeping talents were best served in the banking business, and having always done what his father advised, Dad went to work for the bank without resistance or discussion.

With a population of about eight hundred, Quarryville was the most populous town in the Southern End of Lancaster County. I know that not only sounds small, it *is* small, but compared to the crossroads that essentially defined Rawlinsville, Quarryville was a thriving metropolis. There was pretty much one or two of everything—one main grocery store, two gas stations, two barbershops, one clothing store, one drugstore, one restaurant, and one bank. For entertainment Quarryville had a six-lane bowling alley owned by my Uncle Stoney, as well as two baseball fields. For my mother, who was from the city, the prospect of moving out of Rawlinsville to the big town of Quarryville became her first real dream since moving to Pennsylvania. Her dream came true in 1962, when we moved into a small house on the border between Quarryville and Drumore Township.

Given his experience as a navy storekeeper, Dad had a head for accounting and business, so working for the bank was a great fit. What made it an even better fit was that he was able to develop strong relationships with the farmers and merchants who lived and worked in Southern Lancaster County, as they did business with the Bank of Lancaster County.

It wasn't long before Dad's boss recognized his influence in the community and promoted him to assistant manager of the bank. Of all the things I came to admire about my father, I most admired the lengths to which he went to support the entire working community in the Southern End, including the Amish. As a child, I couldn't know the ways in which he demonstrated his faith in those who came to the bank seeking loans; but I could tell he was highly esteemed from the warm welcome I received whenever someone learned I was Everett Eschbach's son.

By the time I was in high school I couldn't go anywhere without someone telling me a story of something Dad had done for them, and the patience and thoughtful consideration he'd displayed for their financial challenges. Because of that admiration, Dad was given unparalleled hunting access to many of the farms in the Southern End, allowing him to more fully enjoy one of his greatest passions. At least, that's how it seemed to me. We could walk out of our backyard and hunt all day, making one giant circle through the countryside that surrounded our house.

Given my father's reputation in a community so small that everyone knew everyone, I couldn't do anything without being compared to Dad or reminded of how fortunate I was to be his son. Although I never got tired of hearing those things, I'm sure it was a big part of the reason I found so much satisfaction in making my own name running cross-country. In that, there was no comparison to my dad.

Otherwise, I was no exception to the crop of young boys in the Southern End who wrestled, hunted, and trapped during the fall and winter months, trout fished in the spring, and worked in some baseball between jobs during the summer. Unlike most of those boys, though, I was the son of one of the most well-known and respected athletes and outdoorsmen in the area. With that privilege came some wild expectations relating to how I measured up to my father when it came to any of his three passions: baseball, hunting, and trout fishing.

Unlike most of my friends who hunted and fished with their fathers from an early age, my father never took me hunting or fishing with him until I was good enough to do it on my own. That way I wouldn't slow him down. Having been spoiled by three older sisters and a doting mother, Dad never allowed anyone to stand in his way of enjoying his passions fully—not even his sons.

By the time I was good enough to fish on my own, Dad began taking Eddie and me along with him. Although Eddie was three years younger, I was completely responsible for his care when we went fishing. That way Dad could still enjoy his time on the stream without being inconvenienced. So it was always Eddie and me doing our thing, while Dad was somewhere far downstream doing his—avoiding the inevitable task of untangling my brother's fly line from a tree branch.

Eddie never knew a stream in Southern Lancaster County he didn't like falling into. So when he came fishing, I usually ended up giving him my clothes. As much as I hated the cold, it was worse seeing

Eddie cold. Even at that young age, I would have felt guilty not giving up my comfort for his. After the first few times of returning home with only my underwear on under my hip boots, I wised up and began wearing two of everything. Oddly enough, I don't ever recall being embarrassed by how ridiculous I must have looked.

One of my favorite times trout fishing with Dad came each spring when he would allow Eddie and me to miss a few days of school while the trout were especially active. Eddie and I each got our own special day with Dad while the other had to go to school. We'd typically fish from sunrise until about 8:00 a.m., when Dad would leave for work. He would take my catch with him when he left so I could stay behind and start on another limit of trout, and then he'd return around noon to pick me up.

∞

Often on those mornings, Dad and I would fish down in Fishing Creek (pronounced "crick") Hollow. The hollow was roughly three miles through the woods, accessible only by a small dirt road. One spring morning when I was about twelve, I had an experience there that would go down as the greatest adventure of my young life.

I had just finished catching my limit and was sitting beside the creek bank, waiting for my dad to pick me up. Alone in the hollow, I felt safe and at ease. As I waited, I spotted a path through the trees heading up a hill from the dirt road. Believing it was a deer path, I followed it until it ended in a clearing at the crest of the hill. There, I stopped short, amazed at what I saw—a giant teepee.

The campsite surrounding the teepee was littered with plastic milk jugs and clothes hung on a line, and pans and a tin coffee pot lay near a cold fire pit. I was instantly intrigued. I toured the campsite, picking up everything I wanted to study, and soon found myself inside the teepee, stretched out on what I assumed was a canvas bed. I remember having my hands behind my head, legs crossed casually at the ankles, looking up and out through the hole in the top of the structure. Until that moment, I never knew teepees have a hole at the top to allow smoke from a fire inside to escape. I felt like a pioneer—on an incredible adventure, free from school, free from work, free to do whatever I pleased. I rehearsed in my mind how I would tell my friends about it the next day in school. I'd be an instant celebrity.

Suddenly I heard the sound of something or someone walking through the leaves. Just like that, my elation vanished and a sense of sheer terror overwhelmed me. For years I had heard the story of a hermit who lived in the hills around Fishing Creek Hollow, and it was clear I had stumbled upon his hiding place. It was like finding the Ark of the Covenant. But the prospect of coming face to face with the hermit *himself* scared me beyond words. I fled from the teepee, knocking things out of my way, and was immediately clotheslined by the laundry hanging outside. Back down the hill I scrambled, clearing the stream in what was probably a world-record long jump—especially for someone wearing hip boots.

A steep embankment safeguarded the far side of the stream, and I quickly buried myself in foliage where no one could see me or sneak up on me from behind. Within seconds, the man emerged from the path and scanned up and down the dirt road, looking for me. I realized my fly pole and creel were still lying alongside the creek, but at least for now, they were beyond his view. I was nearly paralyzed with fear, and even today, at fifty-seven, I still get a chill thinking about it.

I continued to watch the man, studying him. He looked to be in his sixties. His skin was tanned and leathery, and he had a gray, scraggly beard. He was wearing an old pair of dungaree overalls with a dirty white T-shirt underneath. Gradually, I realized my breathing had steadied, and my terror was being replaced by something else: sympathy. Though moments before I had feared for my life, I now was lying there feeling guilty for all the things I had that this man did not. I would soon be getting picked up by a father who loved me and taken back to a comfortable home, while he would remain in the woods, alone with the few meager belongings that had seemed such novelties to me a few minutes ago.

I was just about to stand and call out to him to apologize for disturbing his campsite when a small branch underneath me finally gave in and snapped. Even though I was almost completely covered in the brush, the man's wild eyes went directly to mine, and I was again nearly paralyzed with fear.

But before he could take a single step in my direction, something drew his attention away from me. He glanced furtively to his left and then retreated back up the trail and into the woods, out of sight. Seconds later, I heard the unmistakable sound of a car's tires on the dirt road, followed shortly by the sight of my dad's white Pontiac coming around the corner. It was the most beautiful thing I had ever seen. I bolted out of the brush like a rabbit and jumped into the front seat of the car, where I couldn't stop screaming, "Get out of here!" Dad couldn't have been less interested in why I was in such a hurry; he just wanted me to be quiet and tell him where my trout and fly rod were.

When I finally retrieved my gear and was safely back in the car, my emotions overwhelmed me. I cried. I laughed. I hyperventilated. I must have said "*Holy crap!*" a dozen times or more. When Dad finally asked me what the problem was, I couldn't put two coherent words together. I couldn't begin to tell him everything that had happened. I had run the gamut of human emotion in less than fifteen minutes, and had no idea how to describe all that had just transpired. When I finally caught my breath I just sat in my seat, dropped my face into my hands, and began to cry.

After a short while, Dad pulled the car over, put it in park, and turned toward me, reaching out and placing his hand on my shoulder. We sat in that position for only a few seconds before I raised my face from my hands and said I was all right. Alongside the time the previous fall when he carried my shotgun for me, that moment with Dad's hand on my shoulder would go down as one of the nicest things he'd ever done for me.

As the car started up again, I turned my face to my window and thought about what I had just experienced. We drove the ten minutes back home without another word. I took my trout into the kitchen, poured them into the sink, pulled my pocketknife from my pocket, and began cleaning them.

Dad disappeared with Mom into the TV room, and I heard him tell her there was something wrong with me; but aside from her briefly asking me if everything was okay, we never spoke of it. I had come a long way from lying in that tepee, rehearsing how I'd brag about the experience, to the state I found myself in now—unable to talk about it at all.

Later that evening as I lay awake in bed, I remembered that in my haste to exit the teepee I had lost my *Quarryville* baseball hat with my first name and the number three printed on the underside of the bill. The man had most likely found it and was now wearing it. I imagined running into him somewhere or seeing him walking along one of the country roads in the area wearing my hat. I imagined sharing a glance with him as we each recognized the other.

It was a long time before I could fish down there alone again without constantly looking over my shoulder, wondering if the man was secretly watching me. Oddly enough, though, fishing there the very next week with only my younger brother, I felt at ease. Perhaps it was the influence of Eddie's worry-free nature, or knowing I had the responsibility to defend him should anything happen.

Over the next few months my thoughts returned constantly to how I would approach another unexpected encounter with the man. It was the first time in my life I had ever contemplated what I would sacrifice to survive or save my brother.

About five months later, in the fall of that year, my father and I went down to the hollow to fish one last time before hunting season began. As it happened, we ended our morning very close to the spot where the path leading to the adventure of my life began. After all that time, I finally told my father what I had seen earlier that spring, and I asked him if we could walk up the trail so I could show him the teepee. When we emerged into the clearing, though, all that remained of the campsite were the poles that formed the teepee's skeleton, remnants of a campfire, and some scattered rags and plastic bags. I felt a bit uneasy not knowing where the man was, but Dad said he'd likely gone someplace even more secluded, and told me not to give it another thought.

But I did think about it, many times over the years. That man, like the farmer in the general store, would live far beyond his lifespan in my mind, where life lessons reside. In my mind, he continues to inhabit a teepee in the woods around the hollow, reminding me of all the small comforts and interpersonal connections we take for granted. For his sake, I try to be more grateful, and to show more compassion to others, even those I might struggle to understand.

Like all true Eschbachs, I loved to hunt. I loved the anticipation and challenge of the shot, and the feeling of pushing through an almost impenetrable thicket. I enjoyed the physical challenge against the elements. Yet there was one interesting contradiction that hunting presented. On days of bitter cold, it pitted my greatest passion against my greatest weakness—hunting versus extreme cold.

Hunting with Dad added yet another dimension—especially when I was just starting out. Simply put, Dad was tireless, strong, and completely oblivious and unsympathetic to any lack of stamina or toughness in his hunting companions, and that included Eddie and me. In fact, Dad hunted with only a select few of his closest friends, and refused to let anyone go with him who wasn't cut from a similar cloth. In my entire life, Eddie and I only had two friends we even considered asking Dad to take hunting with us. One of them, Ed Wenger, remains to this day as much a brother to me as Eddie, while the other, Dave Wimer, I rarely see, but remains someone I could call upon for anything.

Just as Dad did as a pitcher, he put every ounce of his energy into hunting, not caring whether the rest of us could keep up with him. We would leave early in the morning and hunt until we could barely see our hands in front of our faces. Weather was only relevant if it was unseasonably warm. Otherwise no amount of icy rain, snow, or subfreezing temperatures was enough to keep us from hunting. We rested only on rare occasions, and we ate whatever apples we might find on the ground along the way or whatever was left in Dad's coat from a previous day's hunt. Because Dad had hunted and fished the area his entire life, he knew every freshwater spring from which we could drink.

Once, when I was about twelve, I went hunting with my dad and his best hunting friend, Donnie Wissler. It was bitterly cold, and I was miserable within the first hour. In addition to having the endurance of a greyhound, Dad was more tolerant of extreme cold than anyone I've ever known. I rarely recall seeing him wear gloves—no matter how cold it was—nor did I ever see anything but a baseball cap on his head and certainly nothing over his ears that would muffle the sound of a rabbit or pheasant leaving its squat. It seemed the rougher the conditions were, the better my dad liked it, perhaps because he knew fewer people would be out in the elements getting in his way.

Back then, the only gloves I had were a raggedy pair of used meat cutter's gloves that were too big for my hands, threadbare, and more trouble than they were comfort. More often than not, I took them off and did my best to keep at least one hand warm by tucking it between my shotgun and my hunting jacket. Being left-handed, it was normally my right hand that remained exposed to the weather as it gripped the action on my shotgun. Those cold, early days hunting with my dad were more tests of endurance than bonding experiences. Looking back, I suspect I was nothing but a pack mule for the rabbits and pheasants my dad shot in excess of his limit.

On this day, like most others, we were wading through the most impenetrable thickets you could imagine. Green briars were always the worst because they pierced through my hunting pants and sweat pants with ease. From the first day of rabbit season to the last, the backs of my hands were shredded from the briars, as were my cheeks. Getting hit by briars on (and inside) the ears, lips, and eyelids was the worst, but at least the piercing pain momentarily redirected my attention from how cold my hands and feet were.

Less than an hour into our hunt I was frozen to my core. At some point, as we pushed through the thicket hunting rabbits, my dad saw a squirrel run up a tree. Because I was always much slower to the draw than my dad and his friend, it wasn't unusual for the day to end with me having shot nothing. So, Dad saw this squirrel as an opportunity to let me get something for my jacket other than the rabbits and pheasants I was carrying for him.

I tried to convince Dad to shoot the squirrel himself by saying the briars were so thick that by the time I struggled into a position to shoot, the squirrel would be long gone. My reluctance to shoot the squirrel had nothing to do with wanting to spare its life; rather it had everything to do with wanting to conceal from Dad my inability to deal with the cold. My hands were so numb I could barely tell I was holding a shotgun, and my feet felt like two big clumps of frozen meat. There was no way I could distinguish the safety or the trigger, and at that moment all I wanted was to endure the last few hours of the hunt without embarrassing myself as I had so many times before.

Like always, though, Dad wouldn't take no for an answer. So after a moment of fumbling, I pushed through the briars, put the gun to my shoulder, and pulled the trigger, throwing lead at a squirrel I didn't even see. The recoil of the gun was enough to break what little was left of my spirit, and I began to cry from the pain shooting through my fingers. To my memory that was the first time I ever cried in front of my dad. (The second time came later the next spring when I found that darned teepee.)

I imagine most fathers would have called an end to the hunt at that point, but not my dad. Instead he just walked me back to the truck, although he did carry my shotgun, which, as I've said, was the kindest thing he'd ever done for me. He put me in the front seat, shut the door, and disappeared back into the thicket. He wouldn't return until after sunset. I remember sitting in the truck, shivering like a dog trying to pass a peach pit, feeling like a poor excuse for an Eschbach.

While this might seem selfish, and in many ways Dad was, what I learned most from him at that young age was that in his eyes, being a man meant being tougher than anyone else and being able to thrive in conditions most everyone else avoided and perhaps even feared. I'm not saying that's necessarily a good thing. It simply explains why I approached most things from that time in my life as endurance tests.

My dad's example also engrained in me that if you're going to spend time doing something, especially if you spend a great deal of your life doing it, you need to do it with every ounce of commitment you have.

∽

There were also plenty of seemingly small things Dad demanded be done his way and perfectly, such as the direction in which we hunted a field or a thicket. We had to identify escape routes for our game, the effect of wind direction on which way a rabbit would face in its squat, and whether there were any directions we couldn't shoot. Essentially, we had to think steps ahead of simply flushing out the game. This later served me well in the navy, where being able to anticipate and guard against the second- or third-order effects of a decision was paramount. It also explains why making important decisions quickly and decisively was generally easy for me.

But another great thing I learned from those experiences with my father—something I consider equally important—was that not everything had to be done perfectly or even his way. Some things didn't need to be perfect because they just didn't matter, or at least the return for perfection was not worth the extra effort.

Despite his strict expectations where hunting and fishing were concerned, Dad also allowed me a great deal of freedom to figure things out on my own. I loved being able to decide for myself how to do something—even if it was my first time doing it. If I wasn't likely to harm myself or anyone else, Dad didn't interfere, and such freedom and responsibility at a young age were priceless.

I can now see a direct parallel between my dad's method of oversight and my own in the navy, in the way I allowed those under my charge to figure out for themselves how to run their divisions or departments. And while there were some (perhaps seemingly unimportant) things that I demanded be performed perfectly, others I didn't care *how* they got done, only that they got done. As much as I could, I left it up to my team to decide how best to do their jobs, as long as they proved capable.

While my father influenced me in so many good ways, I also saw one thing in him I didn't want to emulate. As the youngest of five children and having three older sisters who doted on him endlessly, Dad was very selfish at times—especially when it came to his leisure time. Charismatic, witty, and something of a "man's man," Dad loved to have a good time. If something came up prior to his heading home for the day that sounded like fun, he did it. He didn't call home to make sure it was okay with my mother; he just expected her to accept whatever inconveniences it caused her.

I was born on December 1, 1957, just as deer season in Pennsylvania was beginning. Dad had driven Mom over every dirt road in the Southern End trying to induce her labor, and either consequently or by happenstance, it worked. As soon as I was born, Dad was on the phone with his mother, not to tell her he had a son, but to ask if she could have a sandwich ready when he got home so he could eat quickly before going hunting. Dad raced home in time to hunt before nightfall, and then woke the following morning to a blizzard that would keep my mother stranded in the hospital for the next five days.

Around the time I entered junior high school, Dad accepted a promotion and was transferred about fifteen miles up the road to a new office just outside Lancaster. This location put him within minutes of the main office and closer to his friends who worked out of that office. It wasn't long before he was enjoying a very active after-hours life consisting of regular stops for drinks with his coworkers before heading home. Our once-sacrosanct family dinners had all but evaporated—at least with Dad there.

One evening he came home late while we were nearing the end of our dinner, clearly feeling the effects of a few drinks. My mother, finally having reached her limit, laid down the law as I had never seen before. I don't recall everything she said, because my siblings and I scattered to our rooms, but it wasn't long before Dad had transferred back to Quarryville and our home life returned to normal. Mom may have been the devoted and accommodating wife, but she showed grit when pushed too far.

But in spite of Dad's selfishness, at his core he was a man who deeply loved his family. He was someone whose eyes spoke the loudest. Never able to verbalize his deepest feelings of love or approval, he had a way of looking at you that said everything that needed to be said. Whoever said our eyes are the windows to our souls must have known my dad. Although he never made much money, he managed to provide a comfortable home, as well as whatever else we needed. Unlike some of my friends, I never had to buy my own clothes in high school, and whatever I needed for running, baseball, hunting, fishing, or trapping, my dad graciously provided. And even though he rarely expressed his love or respect with words, I knew he was proud of me when I joined the navy.

∽

A few weeks after my college graduation, in May of 1979, Dad became mysteriously ill, almost overnight. Over Memorial Day weekend, while playing volleyball in the alfalfa field behind our house, he stepped in a groundhog hole and fractured his ankle. A few days later, in response to a local outbreak of polio amongst the Amish community, we went down to the high school to receive additional polio boosters.

That night, Dad fell ill, and over the next few months became almost completely debilitated. Both hips essentially dissolved and were surgically replaced by the fall, with doctors baffled and conflicted over what could be the cause. For the next three years, Dad struggled without complaint to regain his health, but it never happened.

In September 1982 he was diagnosed with cancer and given only weeks to live. I remember receiving notification via the American Red Cross that I needed to come home in order to see him before he died. Although my captain graciously supported my leaving the ship to fly home, I decided to stay for the remainder of our time under way. I was confident that if anyone could beat the diagnosis—or at least live longer than expected—it was my dad.

For the next thirteen months, Dad went through every treatment, procedure, and operation without complaint. He handled his pain in silence, and he showed me how to die with courage, dignity, and humility. I wasn't able to spend much time with him during that last year of his life, but I was never more proud to be his son than during his illness. Dad's endurance through that time became my touchstone for how I should face my own surgeries and pain.

When he died from leukemia in 1983, the line stretched out the door of the funeral home for more than an hour after official viewing hours had ended. The service was filled with story after story of things Dad had done for those who had come to pay their respects. Like everything else in Dad's life, he had kept those things to himself, never sharing with any of us the risks or sacrifices he had taken for others. It was really a beautiful tribute to the influence he'd had on so many people in the Southern End.

I recall standing at his memorial service feeling both blessed and sad, then thanking God that I'd had a father whom I had loved for twenty-five years, knowing that others would never have that good fortune. Although I loved Dad as much as any son could love his father, I felt more than a little cheated that he'd never had it in him to share with me those secrets of life that only reveal themselves with time. Over the course of my youth, we'd spent hundreds of hours together hunting and fishing, yet he never once verbalized his thoughts beyond wishing me a *Happy Birthday* every December first, typically as we walked alone in the darkness to our deer stands.

In the week before his death, my mother asked Dad if they could talk about their life together. I assume she was looking for some affirmation that she had been the best wife he could have ever hoped for. But even with death plainly in view, Dad couldn't bring himself to open up about the things he held most dear. I know that slight has stayed with my mother through the thirty-three years since his passing, and I also know, had he granted her the words of love and adoration she richly deserved, they would have comforted her through some of the dark times that followed his passing.

During my career in the navy, I not only learned many things that only time can teach, but I also *realized* many things that only time and experience can reveal—things about my youth and the influence of the Amish community in which I was raised, as well as the influence of my family and the adventurous life I was free to live as a young boy. I learned how all those influences guided me through a lifestyle vastly different from the one I'd known growing up.

Decades later, during the darkest time of my life, I sat next to my father's headstone seeking the kick in the pants I needed to get my life back on track, and he provided it in just a few words. Typical Dad.

CHAPTER THREE

MY BROTHER

I couldn't have been more fortunate when it came to my siblings, Marion and Eddie. While Eddie was my best friend and constant companion for many of my youthful adventures, Marion's beliefs and example came to influence me greatly. In order to respect Marion's desire for privacy, I'll simply say I'm extremely proud of her and look up to her. During the toughest times in my life, she was there to give me the harsh dose of reality I needed to keep moving forward and not feel sorry for myself.

Eddie was a wild man from the time he learned to crawl. Once he was old enough to notice me running through the woods and fields around our house, there was no stopping him from coming along. Everything he saw me do, he did faster and with reckless abandon. He climbed trees like a squirrel, raced everywhere without the slightest concern for his footing, and fearlessly crawled into holes under hillside rock formations without giving one thought to the potential adverse consequences. Like Dad, Eddie seemed oblivious to both pain and freezing temperatures. Due to his fearless nature, he was forever sustaining injury after injury that required stitches or special attention from my mother, who was thankfully a registered nurse. Our parents often described Eddie's behavior as "rip, shit, or bust"—meaning storm in and don't think about the consequences.

By the time he was a teenager, Eddie accepted every daredevil challenge from our friends, and never once acknowledged afterward that attempting the stunt had been a bad idea, no matter how miserably he failed or how physically torn-up it left him. In Eddie's case, ignorance truly was bliss. While I was more the type to say, "Stand back, it's gonna blow," Eddie was the type to say, "Jesus Christ, Alan, don't be a sissy." And then he'd rush right in.

∽

Trapping was one of my earliest childhood hobbies. Unlike hunting, for which you had to be at least twelve years old, there was no minimum age for trapping. Eddie and I started to trap shortly after Eddie entered the second grade and I the fifth, making us six and almost nine respectively. One of my father's friends, John Sensenig, taught us how. John was as revered in the local trapping community as my father was for his hunting and trout-fishing skills. John could catch even the most elusive furbearers without breaking a sweat.

During the fall of 1966, John shared his trapping secrets with Eddie and me at every opportunity. He taught us how to recognize evidence of the animals we would be trapping. John could look at the landscape around a stream or in the woods and see in his mind exactly what the animals were doing under the cover of darkness. He would point out little signs of their presence, knowing their meaning and the direction of movement they suggested. He could see things that Eddie and I were unable to visualize.

John was extremely generous with his time, his trapping equipment, and most meaningful, his trust and secrets. By the end of that winter, Eddie and I were as successful as most adult trappers in our community. Although Dad drove us to a few of our trapping haunts, most of the time we were limited only by how much we could carry on our bikes.

For those first few years, setting the traps was quite a challenge. Both Eddie and I were well under sixty pounds at the time, so I would stand on the traps' levers with my heels and push myself down by pressing against a tree while Eddie tried to set the pan in place. That poor kid had his fingers caught regularly, but he never cried or complained. He just wanted to get the trap set so we could catch something.

Each morning after the season began, we'd be up well before sunrise, riding our bikes through the dark countryside to check our trap line. One cold morning, Eddie and I ran into trouble right from the start. We were riding down the hill on Oak Bottom Road, just a few hundred yards from our home. Eddie, as usual riding head down and all over the road, was ahead of me when we hit a patch of ice. It hadn't rained the night before, but the fog must have settled and then frozen on the road surface. Eddie went down first and immediately lost his grip on our .22 caliber rifle that he always insisted on carrying. Being behind Eddie, and because there was virtually no moonlight or even ambient porch light from a nearby house, I ran right into him and was launched straight over my handle bars, face and hands first onto the road.

Being Eddie's self-proclaimed keeper, I gathered myself off the road and immediately went to make sure he was all right. Not surprisingly, Eddie was already on his feet searching the roadside for our rifle, completely unscathed by the fall. I pulled a flashlight from the canvas backpack I wore and handed it to Eddie so he could find the rifle.

By then I'd realized my face was stinging from my face-plant on the road, but I didn't think much of it until I noticed a cold sensation electrifying one of my front teeth. I told Eddie to shine the flashlight on my face as I grimaced widely for him. Eddie barely made issue of what the flashlight revealed, simply saying, "Yep. You knocked one out." Then he went back to searching for our rifle. We eventually found it, collected our bikes, and continued riding off to check our traps.

The first group of traps we checked were those we had set for raccoons. John insisted that when trapping for raccoons, all our sets had to be made in the water. For John, the only way to trap was the responsible way, which meant setting our traps in a place that would give us almost perfect odds of catching only what we sought, and nothing else, such as a hunting dog, feral cat, or skunk. Other trappers, including my friends, were not nearly as discriminating as John, but we much preferred to catch nothing than to catch an unintended target. So even though it took more time and care to make the sets the way John had taught us, that's exactly what we did.

The ideal technique for trapping raccoons involved first finding a small stream in the woods, for two reasons: first, animal tracks are easy to see along streams, with raccoon tracks being among the easiest to distinguish, as they look like small handprints. And second, the tree roots that extend through the ground and under parts of the creek bank serve as obstructions to snag the traps.

Each of the furbearers we trapped reacted differently to being caught. Not to be too graphic, but a raccoon will pull relentlessly to free its leg from a trap—even if that means pulling until its leg rips off. Therefore, traps set for raccoons could not be staked to the ground. Staking them would allow the raccoons to pull against solid resistance, increasing their odds of getting free. Instead, we wired our traps to fallen tree branches we found along the creek, so when the raccoon pulled on the trap, the branch would move with it. John called these branches *chogs*. We never asked John if it was a combination of the word *log* and something else. We simply adopted the word as our own. Using it made me feel like a seasoned trapper when I talked about trapping with my friends at school. The tree roots came into play as the raccoon pulled the trap. The chog would follow along behind it and ultimately catch among the roots.

On this morning, as Eddie and I approached our first set, we noticed immediately that the chog wasn't where we'd left it. That meant we had a raccoon in our trap, so now the challenge was finding exactly where the raccoon was. We walked up the stream until we saw some tree roots, and, sure enough, our chog was right in front of the first hiding place we explored. Eddie knelt in close to shine the flashlight up under the roots, and found the raccoon as far up in there as possible.

Typical Eddie, he had to get as deep under the bank as he could in order to better observe the raccoon. He was almost completely out of sight when I heard the animal hissing, ready to tear into him if he got any closer. My *Stand back, it's gonna blow* mentality went into full throttle as I hauled Eddie out from under the creek bank.

By now my mind was racing in search of a solution to our problem. With Eddie intent on getting back in to the fight, I finally just pushed him out of the way, grabbed onto the chog, and began backing out of the water to bring the raccoon into the open. "Don't shoot until it's in the clear!" I instructed Eddie.

Unfortunately, in my haste to keep Eddie from crawling back underneath the bank, I hadn't verified my footing, and was now doing exactly what Dad and Mom considered *rip, shit, or bust* behavior. Before I knew it, my heel hit a rock, and I fell backwards into the icy water. Maintaining my grip on the chog as I fell, I brought the raccoon completely out from under the tree. I wasn't so lucky when it came to holding on to the flashlight. My butt had barely hit the water when I realized the raccoon was thrashing around wildly between my legs—inches away from that part of my anatomy I had yet to discover any real purpose for. As Eddie yelled at me to get the flashlight back on the raccoon, I flailed at the animal with my feet, trying to keep it from tearing into what little manhood a fifth grader has.

I have no idea how I had managed to find and get a grip on the flashlight, but I had no sooner illuminated the raccoon than I heard the crack of our .22 caliber rifle. Aside from a few death kicks, the raccoon went still instantly. It wasn't the perfect shot between the eyes we preferred for raccoons, but it was in the head. Eddie was only in the second grade.

I gathered myself up out of the water and bent over at the waist, bracing my hands on my knees and wondering what in the heck had just happened. It wasn't even 6:00 a.m., I had been out of bed for less than an hour, had already lost one of my front teeth, come seconds away from being mauled by a desperate, pissed-off raccoon, and escaped being shot by my brother by a matter of inches. My clothes were soaked from the icy cold water and we still had more than a hundred muskrat traps to check. Quite a morning for a fifth grader, I'd say. Eddie was safe, dry, and completely oblivious to the danger we'd been in. And Mom and Dad were probably sound asleep back home. As we rode our bikes from the woods to the pasture where our muskrat traps were set, I once again felt the sting of cold air on what remained of my broken tooth. I passed the time riding wondering what Mom would say when she saw that one of my perfectly straight front teeth was two-thirds gone.

∽

Handling guns unsupervised at such an early age was standard practice back then. We would even bring our new guns into school for show-and-tell. I can't imagine that happening anywhere today. But again, that's just how things were there in the Southern End in the 1960s. The setting made for an adventurous life for a young boy who liked the outdoors. And thanks to having a brother like Eddie, it was even more special. When I look back at the days upon days we'd spend in the woods, gillied up looking for deer, it never seemed like the wild adventure it was. That was just how young boys spent their free time.

Over the next eleven years until I joined the navy, Eddie, our best friend Ed Wenger, and I had some of the best times of my life. Most revolved around hunting and fishing, and ultimately were as much fun to talk and laugh about later as they were to experience. On the coldest of those days I'd have to rely on either my brother or Wenger to put Copenhagen in my mouth, because my hands were usually too numb to feel the dip in my own fingers. We did some incredibly irresponsible things during the 1970s that included lots of beer, gunpowder, CO_2 cartridges, and water—simply for the effect. I helped Eddie pick up, butcher, and later eat a dead whitetail buck he found along a road near our home, and I saw him slice open his forearm with a razor-sharp knife while skinning it out. About thirty seconds after seeing Eddie fillet his arm like a bluefish, I said, "You know that's going to need stitches, don't you?"

In typical Eddie fashion, he said, "Jesus Christ, Alan. Are you ever going to stop being a sissy?"

Even today, some forty-five years later, Eddie and I still share what little time we have together in the woods or along a stream. We meet at Ed Wenger's place in Virginia to hunt every fall, and we meet at my mother's home in Pennsylvania each spring to trout fish. Nothing has changed. I still look out for Eddie, he still ribs me about being a sissy, and he's still rip, shit, or bust. It's the perfect brotherhood.

CHAPTER FOUR

GRAMPA

My grandfather, Maynard Edward Colley, was a police officer in Portland, Maine, for more than thirty years and influenced my life every bit as much as my father. When the United States was drawn into World War II, Grampa could have avoided military service, but that was not his way. Leaving a wife and three children, Grampa enlisted in the army and ended up fighting across three continents over three years.

When Grampa returned home, he brought with him impatience, indulgence, violence, and hostility that would play out for years against my mother, her two brothers, Eddie and Alan, and my grandmother. Although he was not a model of restraint prior to his departure for the war, he came home even more unpredictable and angry than before. After brutalizing my grandmother shortly after his return from the war, he moved out of the house to live with his mother until he was able to sweet-talk my grandmother into having him back. Today his diagnosis might be post-traumatic stress disorder, but back then war veterans suffered and struggled alone to regain their domestic footing. Although he saw considerable combat in China, Burma, and Africa, I never once heard him talk about his experiences.

At five foot eleven inches and 160 pounds, Grampa might have been average in stature, but he was a fearless leviathan in our eyes and to his fellow police officers. While his techniques were often untraditional (if not borderline illegal), his results were undeniable. Although he was never suspended from the police force, his defiance and hostile demeanor kept him from ever being promoted to the rank he felt he deserved.

Like my father, Grampa was highly competitive. An accomplished fighter and swimmer, he set the record for the Peaks Island to Portland swim when he was only seventeen. Anyone who has ever swam in the waters off Portland, Maine, will tell you that while the distance alone is challenging, it's the cold water and current that make it even more grueling.

A few years after Grampa's return from the war, he was involved in a horrific car accident that left him unable to walk. He sustained multiple compound factures in his legs, a broken pelvis, and other internal injuries. He spent six weeks in the hospital, split between the Portland General and Veteran's Administration hospitals, before going home.

Upon being told that he would likely never walk again without the aid of a cane or crutches, if at all, Grampa focused every bit of his physical and mental energy on proving the doctors wrong. He had my grandmother take him and my mother to his friend's cabin on the shores of Little Sebago Lake for his self-rehabilitation. Multiple times a day, Mom and Nana would drag Grampa on a blanket to a rowboat. From the side of the boat, Grampa would pull himself up and over the gunwale, and then roll himself onto the deck. Mom would row the boat off shore and then help roll Grampa into the water.

On that first trip out onto the lake, Grampa's legs were useless except for the purpose of trying to drag him under the water. But in typical Maynard Colley fashion, his relationship with the water proved far stronger than the broken bones and mangled muscles in his legs and pelvis. He would spend the next two months slowly and deliberately regaining his strength, all the while finding an emotional respite from the anguish and memory of war. During his rehabilitation, his drinking decreased considerably and he and my mother shared some of their most memorable and meaningful times. My mother saw in Grampa a strong, fearless man doing his best to cope with the things he had endured during his time in combat. That example set the standard of pain tolerance and endurance my mother displays even to this day.

Once he was able to get around well on crutches, Grampa returned to Portland and was soon headed back to work on the police force, albeit desk duty while he continued to recover. On his first morning back on the job, my mother walked to the bus stop alongside him. When Grampa boarded the bus, he reached the top step, turned, and threw his crutches onto the sidewalk, telling my mother to "throw the sons-of-bitches away."

As Grampa regained his footing at work, his drinking increased and it was only a matter of time before volatility and unpredictability returned to the household. Everyone who knew, lived with, or worked with Grampa gave him a wide berth—especially when he had been drinking. Mom's main duty during her school years was to shield and protect her brothers as best she could from their father. My grandmother did her best to protect herself while also doing her part to keep things at home from unraveling.

The years passed, as they always do, and my mother and her brothers left home, married, and had children. From the moment my uncles became fathers, they never allowed their children to be alone with Grampa. I doubt it was because they feared what he might do to them; rather it was based on their well-founded ill feelings about my grandfather's lack of parenting skills. It was only when my mother was going to be there with us that they would allow their children to be around Grampa in their absence. However, my mother knew Grampa would do anything to protect Marion, Eddie, and me, so we were allowed to enjoy his company unsupervised. That access led to some amazing experiences—especially when I was a young, impressionable boy.

Because of the crazy things we did and witnessed while in our grandfather's care, my sister and I came not only to love and revere him, but also to have a healthy fear of him. At least I did. Eddie was too young to spend much time alone with him, so Grampa had less influence on him. Although Grampa's mood was typically easy to read, when he was drinking, he was like a snake: I could never tell if he was going to wrap his arm affectionately around me or if he was about to choke the shit out of me—figuratively speaking. I loved him deeply, but I gave him a wide berth and did whatever he told me to, no matter how much it scared me. The fear I had of him far exceeded the fear I had of doing the things he expected of me, most of which involved a long swim or deep dive in the lake.

As for Marion, she and Grampa shared a special relationship. Although he was unendingly protective of all of us, he was especially protective of Marion. Maybe it was because she was his first grandchild and a girl. Whatever his reasons, Grampa felt he was Marion's natural-born protector, and he seemed to love her like no other person in his life. Marion would sometimes go to Maine before the rest of us to spend time alone with Nana and Grampa. They would pass many evenings just drifting on the lake, talking about life, Grampa no doubt telling her how much he loved her and having her there with him. I know for Marion there was no man she admired more or in whose company she felt safer.

Most of our time visiting Nana and Grampa was spent at their cabin on the shores of Little Sebago Lake, about an hour north of Portland, Maine. Those weeks during my youth were priceless. We had complete freedom to swim or roam wherever and whenever we wanted. Friends I had made over the years while vacationing there became my daily companions. We would spend hours in the woods building forts out of logs, sticks, and ferns. We swam and fished during the daylight hours and then wandered the woods and dirt roads in the evenings. It was like being back in the woods in Pennsylvania. And it was during these vacations with Grampa that I saw some of the most incredible things I have ever witnessed.

※

I will never forget one sunny afternoon on Little Sebago Lake when Marion and I were with Grampa in his boat. While on the lake, we would water ski, swim off the end of a sandbar, visit one of his police buddies, or just sit somewhere at anchor. Often we would stop at the only place on the lake where you could get fuel: a long pier with a gas pump on the end. Because there was only one station from which to refuel, those in line would wait their turns fifty yards or so from the pier. Everyone knew his place in line, and if someone forgot, the rest wouldn't hesitate to set things straight.

On this day as we approached the gas station, the boat alongside the pump was just pulling away while a cabin cruiser waited its turn to approach. Before the guy in the cabin cruiser could pull in, though, my grandfather zipped right in to the refueling station, cutting off the man without even looking in his direction. The young girl working the station greeted my grandfather with her usual smile, oblivious to the fact that Grampa had ignored the refueling etiquette. The man in the cabin cruiser pulled right up next to our boat and said, "Hey, buddy. Haven't you ever heard of the rules of the road?"

Grampa turned to my sister and me—we were about nine and ten at the time—and asked, "Hey, kids, have you ever heard of the rules of the road?"

We laughed and said, "No, Gramps."

My grandfather turned to the man and replied, "Nope. Nobody here has ever heard of them."

I remember the icy, challenging look in my grandfather's eyes as he stared the man down. The man turned his boat outbound and waited for his new turn without engaging my grandfather further.

We finished refueling and accelerated past the man's boat as if to provoke him further. Perhaps it was my grandfather's way of daring him to do something. Later on we again saw the man out in his boat. Grampa sped up to pull alongside him, telling Marion and me to "wave to the nice man" while he sounded the horn to get his attention. As we waved, I looked over at Grampa to see him grinning in the man's direction while giving him the finger, which he held close to his side in a weak attempt to conceal it from us.

∞

One summer when we arrived in Maine after an all-night drive from Pennsylvania, Grampa greeted us by telling me immediately (before so much as a hug) to go put on my running clothes because he wanted me to race the grandson of another old man he knew at the lake. Apparently the men had been bragging about their grandsons' cross-country skills, each *certain* his grandson could beat the other. So less than thirty minutes after riding in a car for more than ten hours, I was standing next to a kid I had never met before, ready to race six miles for bragging rights between two old men who had nothing better to do than to argue over whose grandson was faster.

The boy I was about to race had supposedly finished tenth the year before in the All New England Cross-Country Championships. I could tell in an instant he was confident of beating me, and by the end of the short few minutes we stood there listening to our grandfathers going over the course, I had already started to dislike the kid as much as my grandfather disliked his grandfather.

I was about to enter my senior year of high school and although I was captain of my cross-country team, I never thought of myself as a great runner. It was just something I enjoyed. Having some teammates who were state champions, I knew what a fast pace was, and I was hoping this kid, although likely fast, wasn't going to be faster than my teammates. More than anything though, I just didn't want to disappoint my grandfather.

The course we were about to run would cover six miles, with the first mile and a half up a steep hill, the middle three miles relatively flat and shaded, and the remainder of the course downhill. Being from Pennsylvania, I was used to running up steep hills, and in fact, if I had a strength that was it. I guessed the kid wouldn't be able to stay with me uphill.

As it turned out, I guessed right. By the time my opponent finished the race, I had been waiting at the finish line for at least five minutes. I shook his hand and heard my grandfather tell his "friend" never to waste his time again. For a moment I felt sorry for the kid. I knew that if his grandfather were anything like mine, he'd get an ear-full on their way home. I remember how proud Grampa looked when he sat next to me in the car. I loved knowing I had his approval.

∽

Very often, early in the evening after dinner, we'd walk around the dirt roads lined with cottages along Little Sebago Lake. I loved these walks with Grampa because he always seemed so at peace. Being beside him made us all feel special. He was handsome, charismatic, witty, loving, strong, fearless, and most of all, protective. I could sense in the way he carried himself that he was proud to be seen with us.

It was on one of these walks that our path took us past the cottage of a man whom Grampa despised. My grandparents had a Wheaten Terrier named Skysail that had gotten into fights with a few of the dogs in the area, including the dog in the cottage we were passing. When Skysail was still in his prime, getting us caught up on the latest dogfights was one of the first things Grampa did after we arrived at the lake. It seemed he never discouraged a dogfight, nor did he guard against them by having Skysail on a leash. Grampa was to Skysail as Don King was to Mike Tyson. If someone else's dog wanted to fight, he was more than happy to let Skysail show the dog's owner what a mistake that was.

So, on this evening as we walked past one of the cottages where Skysail and a German shepherd had done battle, the German shepherd barked wildly at us from behind the screen door. Always the antagonist, Grampa barked back at the dog, further inciting it.

A man came to the door, and I could tell immediately he was coming to scold my grandfather, not the German shepherd. He yelled at my grandfather to stop bothering his dog. Grampa told the man to give the animal to him for an hour and he'd return a well-behaved dog. In response, the man opened his door and told his German shepherd to "sic" us.

With the dog free and running directly at us, Grampa stepped between it and me, prepared to do battle. The dog lunged for Grampa, and in midair Grampa punched it in the head and then somehow got it by the throat and began killing it.

Recognizing their pride and joy German shepherd was no match for my grandfather, the owner, his wife, and his daughter raced outside pleading—screaming—for him to spare its life. Grampa choked that dog until it was completely subdued before picking it up and throwing it into the chest of the man without saying a word. He turned around, blood covering his hand and forearms and already seeping through his T-shirt. He took me by the shoulder and we walked back home. After all I had seen Grampa do, I thought nothing could surprise me, but this took him to a whole new level in my eyes. If there was anything that scared my grandfather, I never saw it.

When we got back to the cabin, Grampa went inside, put on his swimming suit, and waded into the water to relax and clean his wounds. He looked like he'd been attacked by a werewolf. I recall seeing him walking out of the water and grabbing a little chamois he used as a towel before sitting down on the glider beneath the pine trees. I never saw him look at his wounds again.

∽

Most of our days on the lake revolved around swimming and water-skiing. Grampa seemed devoted to teaching us to be fearless in the water, so the daily swim always culminated in a test of courage.

One of the more daunting trials he devised was a deep dive to the bottom of the lake off the sandbar where we often swam. The lake was so deep there that I would completely lose sight of Grampa when we dove down side by side. In my younger days, I would probably make it down twenty-five feet or so before giving up and struggling to swim back to surface. Once on the surface, I would put my face in the water and wait for the sight of him coming back. He always brought a "bottom sample" to prove to me that he had made it. I know the water had to be at least fifty feet deep, and it wasn't until after his death that I ever made it to the bottom on my own.

Often at night, my grandfather would take my sister and me for boat rides, during which he would turn off the engine so we could drift and talk in the reflection of the moon. Although he would often be drinking, he never seemed drunk, and he would tell us numerous times just how much he loved us. Those nights were unlike any others I have ever known.

Sometimes after our talks, as we were heading back to camp, we would play a crazy game of hide-and-seek on the lake, with Grampa and my sister in the boat, and me in the water. When we got about a half-mile from land, it would be time for me to dive over the side and start swimming toward the shoreline underwater. Grampa and Marion would close their eyes for thirty seconds so they wouldn't know which direction I had taken.

My goal was to get ashore without my sister spotlighting me. My strategy was usually to dive straight down and then come up as far aft of the boat as I could. That way they couldn't see which direction I'd gone. After that, the key was staying out of the moonlight and not making any noise when I came to the surface for air. It was exhilarating to be alone in the water at night, watching from a distance as they tried to find me.

One night, I swam far off course and made it to the shore undetected. I was so proud of myself, until I looked back out on the water and saw the silhouette of Grampa's boat in the moonlight. They hadn't moved at all! They were still out there talking and drinking—most likely forgetting I was even in the water. I was about to yell out to them when I got an idea. I'd swim quietly back out and emerge right next to the boat undetected to scare them. I was almost to the boat when I realized I could make it the rest of the way on just one more breath of air. I slid under the surface and almost immediately heard the sound of the engine starting and the whine of the propeller as the boat got under way. I couldn't come up because I was afraid they would run right into me, so I had no choice but to swim deeper underwater until I knew the boat was past. When I surfaced, they were already well beyond me and heading toward the shore. I yelled for them to stop, but they couldn't hear me over the roar of the outboard engine. I watched them spotlight the beach and then head off in the direction of the cabin.

All of a sudden, I was completely worn out. My legs were dead. The fear of being run over may have been a catalyst for the fatigue, or maybe it was the fact I had been in the water for about an hour and had just swum more than a mile. As I watched the stern light on the boat go out of sight into our cove, I felt eerily alone. It was probably approaching midnight, and the lake was completely peaceful and flat. As I started swimming back to the shore, I settled into a comfortable cadence doing the sidestroke, and made it to land without too much difficulty.

I started back to the cabin on foot, and about halfway there, I ran into my sister and grandfather. They had walked the shoreline back to where they thought I'd be. Grampa never thought for a minute that I had drowned. After all, he was the person who'd taught me how to swim. He just looked at me with a little smile that said he was proud of me, and then tucked me under his arm, which said even more. He had a way of making me feel loved and important without saying a word. Marion was Grampa's little darling, and she just said, "Sorry, Al." But her own devilish smile said, "Not really."

I know Marion cherished her time alone with Grampa, and so having some quality time with him on the lake at night was priceless to her. Mom and Dad never knew of our game; it was our secret. But then again, they knew Marion and I were in the best hands when we were with Grampa, so they probably wouldn't have cared anyway.

∽

The years I spent with my grandfather deeply influenced my personality. As ironic as it may seem, given the way he tormented his wife and children, one of his major influences on my life was how he protected his grandchildren above all else. Maybe time mellowed the man, or maybe it was easier for him to cherish us because we were somewhat removed from his daily life. Whatever enabled it, Grampa's fearless devotion to and protectiveness toward my siblings and me would go on to inform how I felt about my own family, and later, my military family as well.

Perhaps even more profound was the influence fearing him had on me. I hated the sensation of doing something out of fear. I found that doing things out of fear had a way of stripping me of my dignity and leaving me without any sense of accomplishment. Consequently for the rest of my life, fear was never a useful motivation tactic to get me to do something, nor was it one I found any value in employing as a leader. I am certain this aspect of his personality is why it meant far more to me that my guys enjoyed the task at hand, than it mattered what the outcome was. For me, it was all about enjoying the experience. I had faith the results would take care of themselves. And they always did.

It was long after Grampa's death that I finally gained the maturity and experience to reflect upon the obstacles he overcame in his life. A father at the age of seventeen, he very likely never remembered a time without stress and responsibility. As a police officer, he chose a profession in which every day on the job could have been his last. He spent three years fighting in a savage war, and then decades battling demons I cannot even imagine. When I think about the love he showed me, the courage he displayed throughout his life, and the influence he had on mine, it saddens me that I was never able to tell him how proud I was of him. In my eyes, Grampa was one of a kind.

CHAPTER FIVE

Coach Harrington

In addition to my community and family influences, sports were also a big part of my life as a boy in Southern Lancaster County—Solanco, as it was known. For me, running was something in which I found incredible satisfaction at an early age, and once wrestling was no longer viable, cross-country and track became my sole high-school athletic focus. Baseball leagues were still a big part of my summers, but running was all I did in high school.

As I would come to realize, the discipline associated with cross-country, coupled with the lifestyle of the community, was a perfect fit for me. I loved how almost everyone else absolutely hated running, and because of the relative ease it posed for me, it gave me a sense of being able to do something most people dreaded. I found incredible motivation in that.

Besides the hard work and, oddly enough, the pain, I loved the clarity of running. It didn't matter if the coaches liked you, or if they happened to be best friends with your parents. If you were one of the first eight guys to run from point A to point B, you made the varsity team. No questions, no discussion, nothing. I also found great peace in the solitude of running and the chance for private introspection. I sometimes ran as many as twenty-seven miles a day, covering the same nine-mile course three times, but I never ran out of things to imagine.

Throughout high school I would get up before 4:00 a.m., run up to ten miles before school, shower, and do my homework before catching the bus to school. I would arrive home after practice at 5:20 in the evening and have ten minutes to get changed and ride my bike to the Sunoco station just down the road in Quarryville, where I would work until 9:00 p.m.

∽

During the summer before my freshman year of high school, I showed up at my first cross-country practice without knowing so much as the name of my new coach. But within minutes I could sense he was unlike any man I had ever met. Art Harrington was in his mid twenties, a former all-state track athlete who was wildly passionate about cross-country. Perhaps more specifically, Coach Harrington was passionate about outworking the competition. Vince Lombardi could have learned much more from Coach Harrington than Coach Harrington could have learned from him, and I can assure you, Lombardi had *nothing* on him when it came to toughness or motivational techniques. I would never say that Coach Harrington was like any famous inspirational person you could think of, because, in my mind, they should all be compared to him.

Running for Coach Harrington was very different from playing baseball for Dad. When I played baseball with Dad either coaching or watching from the bleachers, I was always fearful of making an error or striking out. Dad was not the type to offer encouragement after what he considered a bad game. More than anything, his reaction to a poor performance was disgust—so much so that at times he couldn't even say a word to me on the way home. I could never tell if my performance hurt, embarrassed, or even sickened him. I hated the feeling of not measuring up to his reputation and being an embarrassment to the Eschbach name that was so revered among the old-timers in the Southern End. For Dad, it seemed that results were all that mattered, and effort was irrelevant.

I never felt any of that pressure while running for Coach Harrington. He made everyone feel valued. He had unbelievably high standards for our performance and equally high expectations for our effort. Most importantly, he *inspired* us. Just as John Sensenig had been so giving of his time when he taught Eddie and me how to trap, Coach Harrington put every bit of himself into leading us. Even after he became a father, his wife and daughter would come to our summer practices. He made me want to be a better runner for him—not myself. I loved having the freedom to run without worrying about Coach Harrington losing respect for me, so long as I gave my best effort. He was tough and could be understandably upset at times, but it never felt personal, and certainly never degrading. It was clear to all of us he hated losing, probably even more than my dad, but Coach Harrington's displeasure seemed to be disappointment for us, rather than embarrassment for himself.

Coach Harrington did an unbelievable amount of research regarding the best runners in the state. He did whatever he could to collect information about our competition so that no matter where we went to race, he knew exactly where each of us should finish. In a time when newspapers were the only source for this information, it was remarkable what he was able to put together.

Our practices began in earnest every July and were grueling from the start. Later, when I ran collegiately, I knew with even more certainty just how tough those high school practices had been, as my college workouts never exceeded the level of torture I experienced while running for Coach Harrington. Looking back on it now, I'm sure other high school teams gently worked themselves into shape, while Coach Harrington expected us to come to the first practice having already established a solid distance base on which to build the upcoming season. He would drive ahead of us in his car and tell us our times and splits and whether we were dropping off or hanging tough. Even when he yelled at us, he added just enough wit to take some of the sting off of the stream of profanity. I remember as a young teenager how much humor I found in hearing those words my parents tried desperately to avoid when talking around or disciplining my siblings and me. Like it or not, being called a *little shit* as a ninth grader is far more amusing than it is emotionally damaging. I recall crossing the finish line of a race and being immediately lambasted by Coach Harrington for getting beaten by a kid I should have easily outrun. I was trying so hard not to give him a glimpse of a smirk, but finally I just died laughing and volunteered to start my punishment right then and there.

Unlike some of life's experiences that I didn't fully appreciate until years later, I realized while I was running for Coach Harrington how much I liked him and respected his leadership style. Coach Harrington cared equally about each of us, or at least that's how he made us feel. It didn't matter if you were the best guy on the team, who also happened to be a state champion, or the slowest guy on the team, who was running just to stay in shape for wrestling. He gave every last one of us his time, devotion, encouragement, and criticism. No one got a free pass for a substandard performance, and he could make even the last-place runner feel like a winner if the performance had been that person's best.

Another aspect of Coach Harrington's leadership style I came to appreciate even more when I joined the navy was that he treated each of us differently based on what he knew would be an effective way to motivate us. Some guys could take and respond well to a heavy hand, while others needed a more positive approach. He was too devoted, too passionate, and too energetic to ever adopt a "one size fits all" approach to leading us.

But what I liked most about Coach Harrington, and what I most emulated later, was his sense of humor, which was every bit as effective in motivating us as was his passion. Within all his crazy and animated techniques to get our attention were words, expressions, and mannerisms that were just plain funny. He could have lasted decades as a stand-up comedian using only the stupid things we did for material.

His passion and genuine love for us was unlike anything I had ever experienced. He was endlessly generous with his time, his money, his compassion, and his unwavering belief that we could be the best at what we did. Every time we went to a big invitational, he would tell us that when other teams saw us get out of our van they immediately started thinking about who was going to finish second. I've never had anyone believe in me the way he did, and he was the first of only a few people in my entire life, including Dad and Grampa, who ever truly inspired me. That's the measure of a leader in my mind, and Coach Harrington was certainly that.

CHAPTER SIX

My First True Hero

Because my father's closest sibling in age was ten years his senior, I had only one cousin who was within five years of my age. It was only natural that during my preteen years, my only interactions with my cousins were at family get-togethers, watching them all have fun while my sister, brother, and I did our "little kid" things.

When I was nine, one of my cousins, Davie, graduated high school and joined the navy. Over the course of his enlistment, he was stationed at a small naval base on the Cua Viet River near the demilitarized zone in Vietnam. Davie was an engineman, serving on the small boats that transited up and down the river. I remember sitting on the floor in our den every morning before school watching the *Today Show* scroll through the week's casualties, and how unsettling that was for all of us—especially my aunt, uncle, and Davie's two sisters, Vonnie and Cindy. At the time I was in the fifth grade.

One morning my teacher responded to a knock on the classroom door. After speaking with the caller briefly, she looked directly at me with an expression that's hard to explain now. It instantly told me something had happened to Davie.

By the time she reached my desk, I was already tearing up. The lady at the door took me to the front office, where I waited for my mother to pick me up and take me home. Davie had been wounded, and the details of his condition were not clear—at least not to me at the time. Ultimately we learned his wounds were not life threatening, and Davie returned to full duty.

A few years later, Davie completed his enlistment contract and returned home to Rawlinsville, where he immersed himself in those things all Eschbach men did—hunting and trout fishing. My father truly loved my cousin, so whenever Davie was available, we would hunt together in my dad's favorite spots. Davie became as close to a big brother as I could have ever hoped for. I doubt he ever noticed how I always tried to be close to him as we hunted or sat in the car on the way to our next hunting spot.

On those fall and winter Saturday mornings when my dad was clerking cow sales, Davie and I would go hunting together—just the two of us. I loved hunting with him because unlike going with Dad, we didn't stay out in the elements until we were miserable. We always stopped to have lunch at a country store, and we'd sit down and talk while we rested. I felt so proud to be in his presence.

At the time Davie was working for Uncle Stoney as a bus mechanic. Newly married and with a new house, Davie rarely had more than three dollars in his wallet. It was enough, though, for us to get an egg sandwich and chocolate milk, which he was always more than willing to share with me. On one of those Saturday hunts, we sat down to rest. Having heard so much about Vietnam veterans having difficulty dealing with their experiences, I asked Davie why he never spoke of or seemed bothered by his time in Vietnam. Davie told me all he ever thought about when he recalled his time there was how much beer and Old Grand-Dad were available if you were so inclined to drink it, and how big the rats were. He never dwelled on the combat he saw or the shipmates and friends he had seen killed or wounded—not even years later, when he pulled a piece of old war shrapnel from his face while we hunted. Not until I sat down to write this book did I learn the full extent of his heroic acts on the day he was wounded, the horrific things he saw, and the close friend he saw killed.

To this day I admire how that time in his life, although important, is not something he feels compelled to tell anyone about. He's a typical Southern Ender who works hard, is honest and generous, adores his family, and loves to hunt and fish. Anything beyond that doesn't matter.

Part Two
Life beyond the Southern End

"Challenges are what make life interesting, and overcoming them is what makes life meaningful."

– Joshua J. Marine

CHAPTER SEVEN

MILLERSVILLE STATE COLLEGE

Even after all the wild and formative experiences I had as a young boy, I approached life after high school with more than a little insecurity. I didn't yet appreciate who I was. Being from a small town so isolated from the suburbs and city, I'd yet to realize how special the life I'd lived for eighteen years had been. I left for a college less than twenty miles away still believing that if I could do something, anyone could—a belief that would often turn out to be false.

Being raised in a household where my father would regularly tell my mother she couldn't buy anything else before payday always made me feel out of place among people with nice cars and college degrees. Even at Millersville State College, I initially felt out of my element, and for my first few years in the navy, I was embarrassed I had not attended a better-known university. I remember a fellow junior officer ridiculing me and asking sarcastically if Millersville was a four-year school.

Today most high school students receive the "What's your plan for college?" speech from their parents at some point. Mine came from my father. He advised me that my three best choices were staying home to work on a farm, enlisting in the navy, or going to Alaska to work on the oil pipeline. The prospect of making fifty thousand dollars for six months of work in Alaska was an opportunity my dad thought was worth serious consideration.

Regularly hearing my dad talk about his time in the navy, I always felt I would join at some point, and I even applied to the United States Naval Academy. I went into my interview for a nomination from a local congressman, and I remember him looking at my SAT scores and saying that I'd be lucky to get into Millersville State. The look of embarrassment on my dad's face is something I remember as if it were yesterday.

My four years in college were enjoyable, but most of my experiences there did little to nothing to change or influence who I had become by that point. I made some good friends, had lots of fun, and continued to enjoy running cross-country and track. However, my experiences with my first roommate presented challenges that began to validate not only who I was, but the real power of a perspective on life that had been taking shape since the day I saw that farmer in the general store—namely, my belief that I was in no way entitled to better cards than I'd been dealt.

I quickly learned that my roommate (I'll call him Dennis) was someone whom no one else would room with. He was widely despised and feared on the small campus. With a muscular build and an air of arrogance and defiance, he was an imposing and intimidating person. His use of drugs and constant irreverence toward everyone and everything caused people to avoid contact and confrontation with him at all costs.

Unhappy about his new, unwanted cohabitant, from the moment he met me, Dennis did whatever he could to make my life in that room unbearable. His antics ran the spectrum from impromptu drug parties in the middle of the night to merging my bed with his to build a king-size bed for his and his girlfriend's enjoyment on weekends I was out of town running. I'd come back to soiled sheets, a dozen high, obnoxious people (almost all girls), and a roommate hell-bent on intimidating me into leaving.

I remember on my very first day living with Dennis, he asked me if he could borrow a dollar. I searched through my sock drawer, finally finding one crumpled up dollar, which I handed to him. Assuming it was to buy something, I was surprised when he pulled out a small square of tinfoil, unfolded it, and emptied a white powder onto our dresser top. He took the dollar bill I'd handed him, rolled it up, and used it to sniff the white powder into his nose.

During one of the many nights he returned to the room long after I'd fallen asleep, I woke and found him standing beside my bed with the light on. He was staring down at me with a crazed look. His fists were clenched by his sides, and he was breathing in and out through his nose, looking for all the world like he was about to start pummeling me. At first I simply told him to knock it off, but he was unresponsive. Then I told him he was starting to freak me out. Still no response. I wondered if he were in some sort of drug-induced trance. Finally, for no apparent reason, he started laughing and walked away.

For all the discomfort it entailed, rooming with Dennis actually helped me make friends with some of the older guys on the cross-country team. They knew exactly what Dennis was like and they felt sorry for what they knew I must be enduring.

I've never felt as if anyone owed me anything, and for that reason I have never prayed for God to grant me some wish or relief—not even for my children. Up until college I had never prayed for a good grade, a good race, a base hit, or anything else for myself, so expecting more out of a roommate was something that never crossed my mind. I also never thought about moving out. Things were as they were, and that was it. Looking back, I imagine he was as frustrated by me as I was by him—in his case, for my refusal to be pushed out. It didn't occur to me until later that he'd wanted the room for himself and his girlfriend; I just thought he was an asshole.

Prior to rooming with Dennis, I had never even smelled pot, but living with him exposed me to drugs I had never even heard of—let alone seen or tried.

A typical Sunday evening in college ended with Dennis returning to our room with a shopping bag filled with his next load of drugs. I remember the bag's handles being what I knew as baling twine, and inside was what appeared to be a part of a bale of hay, some baggies with pills inside, and perhaps fifty or more squares of aluminum foil. Dennis would push our big wooden desks together in front of the window, spread newspaper across both desktops, and then place the bale of pot on the desktop. At first I would leave and go to a friend's room, but after a while, we actually began talking while he picked out the stems and seeds from the pot. Dennis would then fill a plant sprayer with grain alcohol and red food coloring, and spray the pot. He explained the coloring would give the weed a reddish tint, enabling him to sell it as Columbian Gold, which fetched more than twice the going rate. When he wasn't high or acting strange, I occasionally found him to be a nice guy. I think he appreciated me not judging him.

As unbelievable as it sounds, it never once crossed my mind how much trouble I'd be in if the authorities ever raided our room. Dennis did his thing, and I did mine, keeping busy with classwork and running twice a day. He never pushed me to try his drugs, and he never bothered me about anything beyond trying to make me so miserable I'd leave.

Dennis had one ritual I found very curious and unusual. He loved the outdoors and found incredible peace sleeping under one of the evergreens in the university president's yard, which was adjacent to our dorm. He'd come into our room late at night, grab his sleeping bag, and say, "See you tomorrow if I don't freeze to death."

Off he'd go, wearing his shorts, white muscle T-shirt, high white socks, and boots for a night under the canopy of evergreens. Rising early for cross-country practice, I'd always give a quick glance under the tree as I ran by to see if he was there. The evergreen branches came down to the ground, so he was completely concealed from the casual passerby.

Just before Thanksgiving during that first semester I roomed with Dennis, we had an early winter storm that dropped about four inches of snow on campus. I remember walking up the few steps to my dormitory when I noticed some books scattered in the snow and what appeared to be a body behind a bench just to the left of the main entrance. The people walking ahead of me gave the body glances of varying degrees of indifference. No one stopped to see if the person was alive.

As the bare legs of the body came into view, I knew instantly it was Dennis. Now I understood why everyone who had passed him couldn't have cared less. I knelt down to check his pulse, left my books on the snow-covered bench, and lifted him onto my shoulders in a fireman's carry. I carried him up the three flights of stairs and down the hall to our room, stripped off his ice-packed clothes, and replaced them with a pair of my sweatpants, socks, and a sweatshirt before tucking him into bed. It never crossed my mind to call an ambulance. Given the amount of drugs I had witnessed Dennis take in the past, I assumed this wasn't the first time he'd misjudged his limit and that he'd likely come out of it on his own.

I walked back down to the front of the dorm and gathered his books as well as my own. On my way down and back, I could hear people spreading the word about what had happened and saying they would have left him there to freeze. Dennis had been so rude to everyone in that dorm that the consensus was he'd gotten what he deserved.

He drifted in and out of consciousness for most of the next twenty-four hours. When I came back from practice the following evening, he was finally sitting at his desk. He looked as meek and uncertain as I had ever seen him. He had no recollection of anything that had occurred the day before and asked me to fill in the blanks as best I could.

Following Thanksgiving I returned to campus a few days later than everyone else because the Monday after Thanksgiving was a holiday in Pennsylvania—the opening day of buck season. Upon my return from hunting, Dennis was unusually nice to me and seemed genuinely happy to see me. He even thanked me for carrying him up from the snow. That was when we started becoming friends.

Most of our longer, more meaningful conversations occurred on Sunday evenings when he'd return with his bag of drugs. On those nights as he prepared his pot for sale and we caught up on things, Dennis began to tell me how isolated he felt. He disclosed to me his premonition of dying in a car accident, and told me his wishes with respect to his things in the room, where he kept his drug money, and what to take or throw away before his family had access to the room.

By the end of our first year together, we had become good friends—insofar as two people so incredibly different can be. As we sat in our room and packed up for the summer, Dennis told me I was the nicest person he had ever known, and he thanked me for treating him far better than he deserved. As David Bowie's *Young Americans* blasted from his stereo, which was pointed out of our window for everyone's entertainment, he reached into his stack of albums and handed me the album that had become my favorite of the many he owned—Boz Scaggs's *Silk Degrees*. It's hard to describe what that simple gesture meant to me, but considering it came from a guy who had months before gone to almost any extreme to test my endurance for emotional and social harassment, it was a welcome sign of his potential for human kindness.

After not seeing or talking to Dennis for the entire summer, I was disappointed when he didn't show up for the start of classes the next fall. After a week, though, Dennis appeared in our room, happy to see me but unchanged in his drug habits. The three months off didn't change where our friendship had left off, and the first album we played after getting his stereo set up was the Boz Scaggs album he had given me the past May.

Everything was fairly routine that fall, until one evening I returned to our room after cross-country practice to find a note from Dennis telling me he was leaving school. He didn't give a specific reason, saying simply that he felt the need to find something more meaningful in life. He thanked me for being such a good friend, and for never judging him. Dennis left behind *Silk Degrees* and *Young Americans* from his record collection, and instructions to look in my sock drawer. In the back of the drawer was an envelope with nearly seven hundred dollars inside. That was more than a semester's worth of room, board, and tuition, and it was far and away the most money I had ever seen at one time.

On my long cross-country practice runs following Dennis's departure, I'd think about him and the way our friendship had evolved from that challenging beginning. I hoped our friendship had become as important and meaningful to him as it had for me. I often wondered if he found whatever it was he was searching for, or if he ever thought back to our time as roommates. For all the unfriendly and appalling things Dennis had done to me, his departure saddened me—he'd ended up seeing me as no one else ever had, or even had reason to. Dennis noticed and appreciated a side of me that was nonjudgmental, tough, and unconditionally kind. I missed having someone around who knew that side of me.

I graduated from Millersville in the spring of 1979 without ever hearing from Dennis again. While I had a great four years and enjoyed some wonderful relationships, it's crazy to think how my experiences with Dennis, often not even remotely enjoyable, turned out to be among the most influential of my time in college.

CHAPTER EIGHT

Getting "Hammered" in Newport

In December of my senior year in college, I took and passed the test to attend Navy Officer Candidate School; however, it would be a year before I'd attend OCS in Newport, Rhode Island. Having done well in my training, I was one of the first candidates allowed to choose his initial tour of duty. My research led me to select USS *Pharris* (FF 1094), a frigate homeported in Norfolk, Virginia. Shortly after my commissioning, I returned to Newport in January of 1981 for nine months of training.

I was only about two and a half months into that training when the influence of my youth revealed itself for the first time. Although I had been raised to be honest and to do the right thing, I had never really reached a crossroad that tested my commitment to my personal standards, nor had I ever taken stock of my drinking habits.

The occasion came with my arrest for drunk driving on the night of Saint Patrick's Day, 1981. I had gone out with some friends for a night on the town in Newport. After hours of drinking, I got into my car and headed to the Howard Johnson's just outside of town for something to eat. To be honest, I did that night what I had done dozens of times before—I got behind the wheel of my car without the slightest regard for my sobriety. I guess because I had never been stopped before, and because nothing even remotely bad had happened as a direct result of my drinking, I assumed this time would be no different. But I hadn't gone a mile before I was pulled over on the main road leading out of Newport.

The police officer saw immediately I was unfit to drive, and he quickly took me from the car, handcuffed me, and put me in the back of his squad car for the drive downtown to the police station. I don't recall any field sobriety test or any discussion about what I had been doing. It must have been clear enough I had no business being behind the wheel of a car that he didn't feel the need to waste time with tests he knew I'd fail.

When we arrived at the Newport Police Station, I was led to a receiving officer who had me empty my pockets into a big manila folder. I remember him sealing the envelope before asking me to sign my name across the seal. I know my recollection of these events are suspect, given that I was quite drunk at the time. However, I do recall being unable to make my hand move in order to sign across the seal. That's how drunk I was.

After being checked in, the police officer asked if I would consent to a breathalyzer. I told him I was drunk and that I would be happy to take the test because I believed I deserved whatever the consequences were for my actions. I blew a .21 on my initial test. That was more than twice Rhode Island's legal limit at the time. About twenty minutes later, the officer asked me if I would consent to a second test, and again I agreed without hesitation. That time I blew a .19. I spent the rest of the night in jail before being released first thing the next morning. I walked to my car, which was still parked along the main road in Newport, and drove back to my room at the bachelor officers' quarters on base.

My court appearance was scheduled for the following Monday morning at the courthouse in Newport. Fortunately my classes that morning were self-paced, so I was able to go to court without missing any. The courtroom was crowded with dozens of other lawbreakers. I don't recall what any of the offenses were, but I do remember sitting there, struggling not to laugh at some of the outlandish excuses people made for their conduct.

My intent from the start was to plead guilty, since there was absolutely no question about that, and also because I felt it would be disrespectful to the police officer who arrested me to dispute his account of the situation. Even had I not consented to the breathalyzer, I still would have pleaded guilty. Lying about my offense just wasn't the right thing to do. I felt badly that it had never crossed my mind that night that I shouldn't get behind the wheel of my car. Lying about the facts of the case would have meant giving up more of what little self-respect I had left, and I was not going to do that.

As luck or fate would have it, I sat through every single one of the other cases before I was finally called to stand before the judge. When called, I stepped forward, now alone in the courtroom with the judge, the arresting officer, and the bailiff. The judge read through the charges, which seemed quite embellished to me, but considering how drunk I had been the night of the arrest, I wasn't about to split hairs over what I might or might not have said to the officer. When he finished reading the charges, he asked how I pleaded. I said without hesitation that I was guilty as charged. The judged seemed genuinely surprised, and for the first time he looked at me over the top of his reading glasses. "Did you say you are guilty?"

"Yes, sir. I am guilty."

He declared my guilt, gave me my sentence, and dismissed me from the courtroom. As I walked back down the aisle toward the exit, the judge summoned me back to set aside the suspension of my driving privileges. The rest of the sentence was a one-hundred-dollar fine and an order to attend the Navy Alcohol Safety Awareness Program (NASAP), which I did.

For every subsequent background check I underwent for my military security clearances, I listed that DUI as a conviction, each time explaining the circumstances and never once being denied a clearance because of it. However, about fifteen years after the arrest, as I was again filling out my paperwork for another recurring five-year security investigation, I phoned the police department in Newport to see if that charge had finally been removed from my permanent record. I had no intention of not continuing to disclose the incident; I was simply curious about whether it had been dropped as a result of never having had another charge brought against me. The woman who answered the phone took my information and said she'd look into it and call back.

Half an hour later, the woman called back and said she had no idea what I was talking about. The only record the Newport Police Department had of my incident that night was that I had been brought in, but that the charge was for reckless driving and had been dismissed by the judge. So, as far as the judicial system was concerned, I had never been charged with—let alone convicted of—drunk driving. All I can imagine is that the judge appreciated my honesty and believed I had learned my lesson. I wish I could have somehow sought him out to thank him for his kindness.

When I walked out of that courtroom, I was at the beginning of my naval career, and for the first time in my life I was realizing what my personal standard of conduct was going to be. I also realized that, even in the face of severe consequences, I was going to stand by that code. I had been raised to work hard and to appreciate all that life had to offer, but somewhere along the way, without ever really knowing it, I had committed myself to living my life in the most honest way I could. Knowing how good it felt to live by that code, regardless of the potential adverse consequences, provided the perfect foundation for all that I would come to experience in my life—in the navy and beyond.

CHAPTER NINE

USS *Pharris*

After nine months of specialized training, I reported to USS *Pharris* in September 1981, shortly after the ship reached the Arabian Gulf on deployment. The *Pharris* was a Knox-class frigate, commanded by a man who personified everything I had pictured beforehand of what a commanding officer should be. He was smart, professional, a gentleman, distinguished looking, fit, and strikingly Pope-like in the sense that I felt privileged just to be recognized by him or be in his presence. He was confident without being arrogant, he never appeared impatient, and he never berated or belittled anyone. For me, in that initial exposure to the *real* navy, he was the perfect commanding officer.

With only a few exceptions, the wardroom was a collection of great officers, most of whom welcomed me to the ship immediately. One of them remains one of my absolute closest friends. However, almost immediately my perspective on life made me feel uncomfortable and out of place. For nine months prior to reaching the ship, I had been instructed by young officers whose singular mantra was that it was of the highest priority and importance to be respected—not liked. Yet, there I was on a ship being served my meals, not doing my own laundry, and being cleaned up after by the same people I was there to serve. From my perspective I felt as if earning respect would be virtually impossible; how can you respect someone who can't do anything for himself?

The mantra of being respected and not liked implies that most officers aren't liked, and therefore it's not important. It also implies that you can gain someone's respect without them liking you. I almost never decided that I liked or respected someone on a first meeting. Over time, however, I liked people because I saw things in them I respected. For me, those determinations were either mutually dependent or exclusive. If I liked you, it was because I respected you, and if I respected you, it meant I liked you enough to admit to respecting you. Even if I respected something about a person, perhaps their work ethic, if I disliked every other aspect of their personality, I would never say I respected them.

An interesting aspect of my perspective began to surface, and I realized that if someone wanted to impress me, all they had to do was tell me how big their deer was, or how long their trap line was. While I'm sure it's not evident to those unfamiliar with hunting and trapping, I knew being successful in those endeavors required hard work, discipline, and getting dirty—all aspects of life I respected. Where someone went to school, how big their house was, or how much money they had meant absolutely nothing to me when it came to earning my respect. If their upbringing had exposed them to hard work, that was a darned good start.

My education from Millersville State College actually made me feel more comfortable with the crew than with those in the wardroom. On *Pharris*, I was one of the few officers who hadn't attended a big school. Obviously most had gone to the U.S. Naval Academy, but the rest went to schools such as Tennessee, Texas A&M, The Citadel, and the University of Massachusetts. Mustangs (officers with prior enlisted experience) were uncommon on smaller ships at that time, so I found myself with little in common with most of the wardroom.

Being served my meals remained the most uncomfortable part of being an officer for me throughout my career. It made me feel as if I were condoning being entitled, which was completely incongruent with my life up to then. Obviously I signed up for that by entering the military as an officer, but I had never thought about what it would feel like for someone else to actually serve me. I didn't even take my dishes to the sink when I was done. Someone did that for me, and often it was a person who only days before had been part of the division for which I was responsible. It was extremely awkward for me. After all, wasn't I there to serve them?

That practice of having members of the crew spend time—usually ninety days—working as food service attendants (FSAs) afforded those who worked in officers' quarters an inside look at how the officers really were. I hated sitting at a table with a fellow officer who never said "please" or "thank you" or was quick to complain about the service or meal. I didn't want to be deemed guilty of the same behavior solely by association. I seriously doubt those ill-mannered officers were ever respected, and they were certainly never liked.

Roughly eighteen years later, during my post commander command tour while serving at the U.S. Naval Academy, I had lunch in King Hall with a midshipman who had been a boatswain's mate on the ship on which I'd served as executive officer. He told me I was the only officer in the wardroom whose food the cooks or the FSA had never "tampered" with. I didn't ask for specifics, but I had a pretty good idea of what I'd been spared.

In addition to feeling incredibly out of place as an officer aboard *Pharris*, I was subjected to my boss's continuous verbal abuse. I'm guessing some of the abuse was put on for effect, but because he never thought about my perspective, he had no way of knowing how his abuse would affect his ability to motivate me. In my view, he was a crotchety, angry, middle-aged man, seemingly unhappy with every aspect of his life. His sole source of enjoyment seemed to be degrading and belittling me. He clearly didn't seem to appreciate all he had as a naval officer serving for a man who ended up being one of the best commanding officers I ever worked for during my career.

My boss's days were spent lying on his rack and bellowing obscenities on the voice-amplified circuit that serviced my workspaces. On what seemed an hourly basis some days, he would summon me to his stateroom simply to verbally bludgeon me about one thing or another.

As a new ensign, I knew I had much to learn, but fortunately I had two seasoned chiefs—a Vietnam small-boat combat veteran and an equally hardened senior chief—who every morning would shepherd me off to the chief petty officer's eating area to tell me the day's plan. I loved that special feeling of being invited into the mess for coffee. I wasn't a coffee drinker. In fact, up to that time I had never tasted coffee. But turning down the offer would have made me seem unappreciative of their hospitality and kindness. I think they could see right away I was well acquainted with hard work and was not someone who thought he knew everything simply because he outranked them.

Such kindnesses aside, my rude introduction to sea duty was not going well. Between periods of abuse from my boss, I spent my time in the workspaces with my chiefs and the roughly sixty people that made up my two divisions. I felt right at home during the hot, sweaty hours in those spaces. It was especially hot because our main propulsion plant was 1,200 PSI superheated steam, and we were in the Middle East to boot. It reminded me of my youth working the tobacco fields in Pennsylvania, and I know it was eye-opening for my people to see a young officer actually enjoying that hard, hot, dirty work.

I instantly felt much more at home with my people in our workspaces than I did in the wardroom, and so I started to eat my meals occasionally on the mess decks instead of in the officers' mess. But I found eating with my guys felt unfair given that they didn't have the same option of joining me in the wardroom to eat. As a result, I felt just as out of place on the mess decks as I did in the wardroom.

After roughly one month on board *Pharris*, I decided I had taken enough abuse from my boss. Maybe it was simply the toughness from my upbringing coming through, or perhaps I was hoping confronting him would lead to my dismissal. I wasn't sure at that point, but I knew even then that life was way too short to spend one more day putting up with my boss's unjustified wrath.

After being beckoned to his stateroom for another profanity-laced tirade one day, I decided it was time to take a stand. Fear and intimidation had never motivated me to do anything for anyone else. I'm not saying there aren't things that scare me; I'm just saying that if a person wants me to do something, a tongue-lashing or a threat isn't going to help their cause. Having had the experience with my college roommate and my father's crippling illness, standing up to an abusive boss didn't intimidate me in the least—even as a young ensign. Long before I stepped aboard that first ship, being yelled at was something I actually found comical, but that didn't mean I was going to take it or allow it to be my boss's primary source of entertainment.

On the day I finally took my stand, I knocked on my boss's door, went inside, and before he could start into me, I said, "I just want you to know I am sick and tired of the way you treat me, and from this moment on, I am not going to respond to it."

His response was instant, and I recall it word for word as if it happened yesterday. He said, "Now look here, you little fuck. When you're a lieutenant commander department head, you can treat an ensign any way you like. Now get the fuck out of my stateroom, and come back in the right way."

I looked right back at him and said, "I'm leaving, but I'm not coming back. You can yell for me all you want, but until you talk to me in a more respectful way, you won't see my ass again." I turned and walked out of his room, him screaming at me to come back all the while. Things would have been different had I not been doing my job. But I knew that with the enormous help of my chiefs and my guys, I was doing just fine.

His bullying stopped almost immediately without my stand ever being addressed, and he began treating me very well. I actually started viewing him in a different light, and for the most part, I ended up enjoying working for him. It laid the groundwork for future interactions and gave me the confidence to confront people with whom I was having difficulty working.

My Uncle Alan used to tell me that he wasn't fluent in body language. What he meant was that often in our dealings with people, we make assumptions regarding how they feel or what their intentions are based on our own interpretations of their body language. Misinterpretations can lead to perceived slights or bad attitudes when there are none. So, after my experience with my boss, if I had an issue with someone, I tried to confront them in a direct but nonaggressive and respectful way. I wanted to be sure that if I judged someone a certain way, my views were valid. That approach to confrontation virtually eliminated stress from the dynamics of human interaction for me.

Before long I had a new boss, and immediately my life as an ensign aboard *Pharris* got infinitely better. My new boss was professional, smart, and collegial, and actually seemed to enjoy working with his division officers. Although it was clear whose department it was, he gave us the freedom to decide how best to run our divisions. He recognized the value of the division officer–chief petty officer working relationship, making sure everyone understood how important he deemed it. The bond between the division officers and chief petty officers became the foundation for the division, and made that first division officer tour unbelievably special for all of us in the department. That tour set the standard for how I came to believe all divisions should function.

With the support of my chiefs, I worked incessantly for the next year to complete my Surface Warfare Officer (SWO) Professional Qualifications Standards (PQS). Our recently reported operations officer had made a PQS progress chart, which he posted on the bulletin board just outside the entrance to the wardroom. Unless you entered from the aft side of the wardroom, you couldn't miss it. Along the top on the chart's x-axis were the PQS areas leading up to a finish line. All the junior officers still working on their qualification standards were listed down the y-axis with a horse in each row. I became moderately obsessed (if it's possible for any obsession to be "moderate") with seeing my horse progress toward the finish line.

As the newest reporting ensign, my horse was solidly in last place when the chart was first hung on the bulletin board. Just like in running, I was now motivated to get from point A to point B faster than everyone else. I didn't pass everyone, but I came close.

Every surface warfare qualified junior officer in the wardroom was supportive of the qualification process, and remained approachable so that those of us going through the process could demonstrate our understanding of the many and varied qualification standards. With the help of my fellow ensigns, my chiefs, and the department heads, I completed every requirement for SWO qualification within a year of the day I reported aboard.

So there I was, only a year into my initial tour in the navy, and already the perspective I had formed during my youth had begun to shape how I dealt with my life in uniform. By the end of that year, I had completely lost the feeling of being intimidated by the education or pedigree of other officers, and even my feeling of being out of place in the wardroom had faded. I had found comfort in who I was and had made some great friends along the way. Had I not had the courage to stand up to my boss, or to listen to my own instincts about my role as a young officer, things could have gone much differently.

CHAPTER TEN

BUD/S

Although my tour was now going well, I knew there had to be a better fit for my personality, so I began looking seriously into SEAL training. SEAL is the acronym for "Sea, Air, and Land," and is the Special Warfare branch of the navy. It wasn't *being* a SEAL that intrigued me; it was the challenge of their training that got my attention. I wanted to see if I had what it took to get through it.

After hearing from the SEAL detailer almost weekly for months that there were no spots in BUD/S (Basic Underwater Demolition/SEAL) for officers coming out of the fleet, he finally got tired of my calls and told me to contact a chief petty officer at one of the SEAL teams in Little Creek, Virginia. I immediately phoned the chief and arranged a time to take the SEAL physical fitness screening test.

I reported as directed to the track on the Little Creek Amphibious Base in Norfolk, Virginia. There, I was met by a SEAL chief petty officer and about eight other guys, all there to take the test. The test consisted of a mile run in boots and long pants, a swim of a length I don't recall (but I do remember that the water was *cold*), and some number of pull-ups that wasn't too difficult. It was probably mid-November, so the weather was perfect for running. When we lined up to run, it was like being back on my high school and college cross-country teams, and I could tell each of us was sizing the others up. When the chief gave us the go-ahead to start, three of the younger guys took off like the race was a sprint rather than a mile. By the end of the first lap, they had all but petered out, and when it was over, I had finished in just over five minutes, lapping all but a few of the guys.

By the time we reached the pool, felt the cold water, and were waiting for the signal to begin, about half the guys had decided they'd seen enough and didn't even stick around for the swim or the pull-ups. By the end of the test, there were only three of us getting off the pull-up bar, the rest having drifted away at some earlier point. The chief took notes without comment, giving us no indication of what might be next, and then we left. Whatever the chief thought, it was good enough to get me accepted into the program, and I was assigned to Spring Class 124 in March of 1983. At the time of that assignment I was unaware that I would be the class leader of 124, but it was a role that became one of the most significant of my life. Certainly at that time, it was *the* most significant.

Over the next four months, as I prepared for my class, I courted and married a girl from my hometown who I had always considered way out of my league. Then, in March of 1983, one week after getting married, and after doing virtually no research into what was about to begin, I flew off alone to Southern California to begin my training. Showing up as a lieutenant junior grade gave me the distinction of being the senior man in the class by rank, and I was unceremoniously announced as the class leader the moment my boots hit the compound asphalt. Being named class leader didn't get me any one-on-one guidance from our class proctor on what was expected, so the only way I knew if I was executing my duties properly was by avoiding the thrashings that indicated otherwise.

In life, whether in corporate America or in the military, nothing is held in higher regard than leadership, and that is especially true in Special Warfare. This meant there was much expected and demanded of me as class leader. To be honest, the thought of being class leader never crossed my mind before it became a fact, but like everything else I had done in the navy, I simply put the best interests of the other guys in my class ahead of my own.

During the months leading up to my assigned report date, I worked out more than ever before. I did every run in a pair of Davie's jungle boots from his time in Vietnam, running up to ten miles at a time—mostly through Seashore State Park in Virginia Beach. I did sessions of five hundred or more push-ups in as little as ten minutes, and I did pull-ups on virtually every tree branch, flight deck net, chill water pipe, or playground jungle gym I could find. At six feet tall and 160 pounds, I thought I was in great shape and ready for whatever physical tests were about to come. I couldn't have been more wrong.

I will never forget the first morning I showed up for the pre-dawn physical fitness period. At the time, there were probably about two dozen of us who had reported early, before the official report date. We formed up at the barracks at 4:45 a.m. and then ran over to a field on the amphibious base in Coronado for the 5:00 a.m. physical training session. It was completely dark except for some background lighting from the bay and whatever streetlights were close by. We assembled into a circle and waited for the SEAL instructor to show up.

Seemingly out of thin air, I saw the silhouette of a man, who I guessed to be our instructor, walking to the center of our circle—at least I assumed he would stop in the center. I had no idea where he had come from, nor did I have a clue as to how things were going to get started. Was I to report that the class was ready to go? Was I to introduce myself and ask him out to breakfast? Or was I to just stay quiet and let him figure out on his own that there was fresh meat in the area? It took about two seconds for those questions to be resolved. I don't know how the instructor knew I was new to the class, because, as I said, it was nearly pitch black—but he made a beeline for me and didn't stop walking until his face was less than an inch from mine.

Had the movie *Back to School* been released then, I would have thought he sounded a lot like Professor Terguson (played by Sam Kinison) as he screamed into my face, asking why I was too big of a coward to present the class. From there, he proceeded to lead us through exercise after exercise targeting our abdominal muscles. Some I couldn't even pronounce—let alone find the strength or coordination required to complete them. Ten minutes into the session, I couldn't do one good repetition of anything. I just stayed lying on the ground, unable to even pretend I was doing an exercise. It was pathetic. The worst part was being seen like this in the presence of my new classmates, whom I was expected to lead through training. For as much pain as I was in physically, far worse was the humiliation of having been so effortlessly reduced to a human dishrag in a matter of minutes.

By the time that ninety-minute session was over, I could barely stand. We formed up on the field before running over to the mess hall for breakfast. During breakfast I sat next to one of the other officers in my class, Ensign Rob Monroe. I had met him the day before when I checked in, and he had taken me downtown to get my uniforms and showed me around as much as possible. Rob and I ended up being roommates and quickly became close friends. As we sat at breakfast, he made a joke about the thrashing I had taken, assuring me things could only go up from that moment on. I sure wish he had been right.

After breakfast we again formed up for the run across the road to the BUD/S compound and my next introduction to more of the instructors. As an aside, my detailer didn't tell me exactly when my class began; he just said to show up as soon as possible in March, so that's exactly what I did. I had no idea what to wear, what to say—nothing. So now, here I was, running over for my first appearance in the compound as class leader, naive enough to think that the worst part of my day was behind me. I was rehearsing in my mind how I would present the class this time, having learned that saying nothing wasn't going to cut it.

By the time we entered the compound, I was feeling a little better about myself and the day, as I ran in my green utility uniform, jungle boots from Davie, and a nice black belt. Just as we finished forming up, another SEAL instructor emerged from the building. The second he laid eyes on me, and before I could even open my mouth to present the class, he rushed up to me, grabbed me by the collar, pressed his face into mine, and began verbally thrashing me for being such a pathetic excuse for an officer. He then proceeded to drag me back and forth in front of the class, demanding to know if they wanted this idiot to be their class leader. I had no idea what he was so pissed off about until he finally pointed out that officers wear khaki belts—not black belts. Having never worn a green utility uniform before, someone could have told me to wear a yellow tie-dyed belt, and I would have done it.

If any of my classmates responded to the instructor's jeers, I was oblivious to it. I just knew I had to get that damned belt off as soon as possible. Few things scared me at that point in my life, but being manhandled so easily by that SEAL, that scared me. I may have snickered at being dressed-down by Coach Harrington, but I didn't find this ass-chewing the least bit comical. I think by then, my sense of humor was off hiding in a corner. Still, I took the thrashing in stride and as unlikely as it seemed, things did start to look up from there. Looking back, I'm sure the instructors were happy that I teed one up so nicely for them.

Those next few days of morning PT sessions were agonizing. For most of the first week, my morning began with me rolling out of bed onto my hands and knees and using the side of the bed to pull myself to my feet. But just like everything else, the sessions got easier as my muscles strengthened and my endurance increased. As tough as the PT sessions were, running was relatively easy—especially when we ran for time on the hard-packed sand along the shoreline. Those runs provided the only physical relief I had during the first few weeks.

During that time, I would think back to being on the *Pharris* and being berated by my boss, and I realized how different that was from the verbal abuse I was taking at BUD/S. In spite of the constant onslaught from the instructors, none of them seemed unnecessarily angry. In fact, I could tell there was a purpose in their words, even if that purpose wasn't clear to me.

The other aspect of BUD/S that struck me from the start was that officers were expected to lead from the front and take care of themselves last. The result was a culture very different from what I had experienced on a ship, and I loved it. When we ate, I ate last with the other officers just ahead of me, and also after the rest of the class. When I finished a run, I would run back to encourage the rest of the class.

As I recall, when class 124 finally finished forming up about two weeks after I reported, and began training, there were 103 of us. On the first day we were crammed into a classroom and were advised to look around at one another because roughly 70 percent of us would be gone by the end of Hell Week. This day would likely be the last time we'd get a good look at each other.

I remember once again looking around at my classmates and sizing as many of them up as I could, foolishly forgetting that looks don't mean shit about what someone has inside. Still a little uncertain of myself, and still believing that if I could do something, anyone could, I didn't see too many guys who I thought I would outlast.

The first two weeks of training were focused primarily on testing our physical and mental strength. Unless someone suffered an injury (which was fairly common), everyone had to finish the first two weeks, which were actually described as "pre-training." Each day we would PT in the morning, then run in the loose sand, run the obstacle course, which was a son-of-a-bitch, and then do some open ocean or pool swimming.

Because the class was so big, and the pace of the daily schedule so fast, I had little opportunity to get to know anyone except for Rob. He was from the Pacific Northwest and had recently graduated from Washington State University. What struck me immediately about him was that he had no conceit or arrogance. He was tall, lean, and never seemed overly concerned about anything aside from giving his best to whatever we had to do. I showed up at BUD/S expecting all the guys to be the chest-beating type, and so I noticed right away that Rob could not have been more grounded and humble. Unlike me, who showed up at BUD/S thinking more about taking on the training than what it would actually be like to be a SEAL, Rob had known he wanted to be a SEAL for many years. Even though most days we only got to talk during meals, it was nice to know I was going to be sharing those days with a friend.

The first time we ran the obstacle course, the instructors told us to bypass three of the most difficult obstacles: the sky scraper, the slide for life, and the cargo net. I'm guessing the reason was that until we improved our strength, there was a good chance we would get hurt by losing our grips and falling. Each of our next three times on the course they added one more of those obstacles until, by our fourth time, we were running the entire circuit.

The slide for life (a misnomer by the way—there is hardly any sliding involved) is essentially a rope tied between two poles of different heights. The first pole (the higher of the two) is a telephone pole you climb up until you reach a platform. Standing on that platform, you reach out, grab the rope, and swing your legs up and around it, looking like an inverted inchworm as you make your way down to the lower pole. Trust me, it's much harder than it sounds, especially at that point in training, when your muscles are cramped and sore and you know nothing about technique.

I remember my first time climbing up the slide for life, my forearms were already so sore from the first half of the obstacle course that I could barely make a fist. That initial trip down the rope must have taken me five minutes. I wrapped my legs so far around it that the outside of my right shin was flat against the rope with my left leg wrapped over that. Every time I inched (and I do mean *inched*) farther down the rope, I could feel it burning and tearing the flesh off my right leg, just above my boot. By the time I finished the slide for life and the rest of the course, I had a third-degree burn on my leg the size of a silver dollar. I finished that day without looking at my leg again. It was like avoiding checking the oil in your car when you know it's going to be black, and you'd rather not confirm what you already know.

When I got to my room that evening after dinner, my leg looked like burnt hamburger and was already starting to get infected. Rob drove me to the pharmacy, where I bought some gauze bandages, medical tape, and zinc oxide. For the next month I stayed as far away from sick call as I could, because when someone went to sick call, they typically didn't come back. I tried some of the craziest home remedies I could think of, but nothing worked.

Because we spent so much time in the water, my leg would not heal. Fortunately, most of first phase was spent in long pants, so unless we were in the water wearing only our UDT swimming trunks, no one could see the ugly mess on my lower leg. I took the bandages off every morning and cleaned the wound one last time before heading out for the day. When we were on the pool deck or getting in the ocean, I stood in a position that would keep my leg from being noticed. As Hell Week approached I started to worry that without being able to tend to it each evening, it would likely get infected and the instructors would roll me back to the next class to restart training.

The month after pre-training and before Hell Week was a blur. I'm sure I was given extra attention because I was the class leader, just as Rob and the other officer in the class were getting their own special attention, but I don't recall anything in great detail. I just know our tolerance of the cold was constantly tested through open ocean swims without wetsuits, and our fitness stressed to ever-increasing heights. An event known as "night rock portage" was grueling, but it was so chaotic I don't recall much about it, aside from being so physically drained afterwards I was hallucinating by the time I phoned my wife later that night.

Being a decent runner was a real plus at BUD/S. Although everyone's times improved in the weekly two-mile swim and obstacle course, people are typically limited in their abilities to dramatically improve their relative standing in running. And as I knew from running throughout high school and college, running for time sucks. There is no way around that. So during that first month, while many of the guys struggled with running, for me it was actually the only time during training when I felt I was able to catch a break.

One of the biggest benefits of being class leader was that I couldn't hide from the instructors. I know that sounds counterintuitive, but it allowed the instructors to truly get to know me, and fortunately, with the exception of just one of them, they all ended up liking me quite a bit. As class leader, I was not only given special attention, but was also subject to higher expectations—ones I fully understood and embraced.

Every morning during first phase, we would assemble by a loading dock on the Coronado Amphibious Base for our physical training session. In the weeks preceding Hell Week, two SEAL instructors would attend the session, with one leading the exercises while the other walked around, ready to pounce on anyone who couldn't keep up. When that happened, the instructor would order the trainee to run to the nearest body of seawater to "get wet." In fifty-six-degree water, it wasn't a whole lot of fun. As class leader, I had to run along with each of my classmates who had been ordered to get wet. Because those first PT sessions were the most physically challenging thing I had ever done, there were times I couldn't wait for one of my classmates to be ordered into the water, because running to and from the surf zone gave me a little break from the pain. Even though I, too, had to jump into the cold water, it was far less grueling than the physical training.

After a while, the instructors caught on and ordered me to remain behind while the guys were sent to the water on their own. We would do hundreds of sit-ups (as many as 750 straight after Hell Week), back flutter kicks, good-morning darlings, and the one exercise I never mastered: sitting twisters. The instructors finally just started telling me to get wet when the next exercise was sitting twisters. It actually became somewhat comical.

As Hell Week approached, the soreness from those morning PT sessions was gone, and it wasn't long before all of us in class 124 began to see a transformation in our bodies. Whenever we were preparing for an evolution in the pool, we had to remain just outside the locker room, downstairs from the pool deck, until we were cleared to come topside. The leading petty officer (LPO) of the class and I once noticed how defined our chests and abdominal muscles had become, so as we waited for the instructors to call us up to the pool deck, we would pose and flex, admiring our reflections in the windows. It didn't take long before everyone in the class was pushing to get past us so they, too, could get a clear view of their own reflections. The transformation seemed to happen overnight, and noticing that change was a great source of amusement for us.

Every Friday afternoon, just after lunch, I would go to my class proctor (the "good cop," so to speak) and get the schedule for the following week. Because of how overwhelming and intimidating the weekly schedule was if you looked at it in its entirety, I was directed not to share the day's schedule with anyone other than our class LPO until the night before. Since Rob and I were roommates and good friends, I did share the schedule with him. Initially it was easy to look at it and think, *Oh, that doesn't look too bad,* only to find out later that even the most seemingly benign, low-key evolution on paper was a raging tiger in execution.

One time during an evolution that looked and sounded much harder than it actually was (it involved trying not to drown), one of my instructors became especially animated over the performance of one of my classmates. If you've ever seen any documentary about BUD/S, it included an event in the swimming pool known as "drown proofing," during which your hands and feet are tied together behind your back. The evolution consists of coming to the surface for a breath of air roughly twenty times and then completing a one-hundred-yard swim while bound. Although I, like most of my classmates, found this to be one of the easier evolutions, it was one that was a little unnerving to watch prior to getting into the water. In execution, all you really had to do was relax, and it was no problem.

This evolution occurred during the weeks preceding Hell Week, so a number of guys were still struggling with some of the physical and mental challenges. Unfortunately, during drown proofing, one of the guys panicked the moment his feet hit the water. Every time his head broke the surface, he would scream a word or a syllable until he completed the sentence "I CAN'T DO THIS." One of the instructors had a shepherd's crook that he would shove into the kid's chest or forehead every time he broke the surface, while telling him that he was, in fact, executing the task.

Our instructors typically didn't tell us how to get through an evolution. They tended to let us struggle through and either figure it out on our own or fail. But in this case the instructor just kept telling my classmate to relax—at the same time calling the attention of the other instructors so they could enjoy the show. Moments like this allowed the rest of us to cut some corners without being noticed by the instructors. A person struggling in the water caused a feeding frenzy for the instructors. They lost track of everyone else as they competed for who could make the funniest remark about the flailing man.

I have to say that in my experience, SEALs are universally recognized as being among the most highly trained warriors in the world, but what rarely gets acknowledged is how damn funny they are. In the midst of the constant harassment were some ridiculously comical times if you had the wherewithal to recognize them.

All of our instructors demonstrated confidence without a hint of arrogance. These guys knew who they were and couldn't have cared less what anyone else thought. If there was something they feared, they never showed it, and I never saw them angry. Even when they yelled at us, I knew it was fun for them, and it became even more entertaining if it flustered the class into doing something stupid.

∽

During first phase, every week ended on Friday afternoon with my class sitting in a classroom with our proctor. This boatswain's mate chief was a riot. He would stand in front of the class and tell the most amusing (and somewhat unbelievable) stories. While I can't remember them all, I recall that many of them had something do to with the unfortunate, uncontrolled defecation experiences he had while parachuting, or while afflicted with some obscure tropical parasite.

The role of "class proctor" was a confusing one for the trainees to grasp. On paper the class proctor was the SEAL on the BUD/S staff who oversaw the schedule for the class. During each phase, a different instructor would be assigned proctor.

The first-phase proctor was unique in the sense that during first phase, especially prior to Hell Week, we were constantly being harassed. Some of the instructors were better at the art of toying with the trainees than others, and I always considered the best instructors to be the ones who were absolutely brutal in their harassment of us, but at the same time hilarious in their comments, expressions, and antics.

In this, my first-phase proctor was in his element. The other instructors were forever reminding us how fortunate we were that our proctor was forced to play the "good cop"—the one whose job it was to pick us up rather than to constantly tear us down. I could tell right off he was the best at every form of physical and psychological harassment imaginable, and I was thankful to have him on our side—at least a little bit.

One of our proctor's funnier routines involved him coming up behind one of us during an event that he wasn't part of and trying to lure us into a casual conversation. Inevitably, one of the other instructors would catch us saying something out of line, or see us relax just a little too much, and would immediately pounce on us. As he walked away, our proctor would say something like, "Oh, shit, Alan. I'm sorry. I didn't think they could hear us. Looks like you're really screwed now."

Right off the bat, he started calling me "Alan," which I loved. In the military, juniors don't call seniors by their first names, but my proctor, and every other instructor for that matter, had positional authority over me, so I considered all of them senior to me even if a navy pay-grade chart indicated otherwise. After Hell Week, when we were allowed to dip or chew tobacco, our proctor would ask me for my Copenhagen. After he had pinched up, he would spin the can between his thumb and index finger as he told us story after story. I think most of the young guys just wanted him to shut up so they could begin their weekend, but I never tired of his stories. He would stop in the middle of a yarn, look at me, and say, "You're wondering when I'm going to give your Copenhagen back, aren't you, Alan?" I always laughed and invited him to keep the can, which he never did, always placing it on my desk as he walked around the classroom.

Once dismissed for the weekend, Rob and I would head back to our rooms in the BOQ. On our way up we'd stop by the beer machine and buy two beers each—Michelob for Rob and Budweiser for me. Then we'd retire to one of our rooms to sit and reflect on the week and life in general. During one such conversation, I was reminiscing about my boss on my first ship, and I realized that perhaps at the root of his anger was fear or insecurity. He was a short man, and a bit overweight, so maybe that played into it. Or it could have been that as the engineer officer, he'd felt less qualified than some of the other officers with more traditional mariner skillsets. Whatever his reasons, I began to suspect that lashing out was his way of coping with his insecurities. In contrast, my SEAL instructors, who surely had things to be anxious about, were confident enough in who they were and what they could endure, to not be intimidated by their own vulnerabilities or shortcomings. It was a quality I admired. Seemingly overnight I found my own demeanor reflecting that same unassuming self-confidence—one that acknowledged my insecurities, but wouldn't allow those insecurities to stand in the way of what I had to do.

CHAPTER ELEVEN

HELL WEEK

More than two months after arriving in California, Hell Week was finally upon us. The number of people in my class had dropped from 103 to 74 during the month leading up to it. The week before Hell Week was different from the others because it was filled with anticipation. Even when Hell Week wasn't being talked about openly, we knew it was coming, and it loomed over us like an ominous, evil entity. It was as if a storm were brewing and people were gathering to watch the destruction.

As much as some guys dreaded Hell Week, I just wanted it to start so I could find out what all the hype was about. At the end of every day during the week before, our proctor would say something like, "What's going on next week? Is it gosh-darn week or something like that? What the hell is it?" Even our instructors seemed to ratchet up their abuse of us, as if they were honing their skills.

That last Saturday before Hell Week, we spent hours setting up a huge tent. And on Sunday, we bedded down in there, unable to really sleep, anticipating but not really comprehending what was about to start. Around midnight, someone came into the tent and herded us outside into one of the drying cages behind the compound. We knew we were about to "break out"—the term for starting Hell Week—but we didn't know what the cage was for. And then, just as that instructor did on that first dark morning

I went to PT, the SEALs slowly materialized out of the darkness, coming from every side of the cage. Simultaneously, they opened fire on us, blasting our class with a fire hose, machine gun fire (with blanks), percussion grenades, smoke grenades, and lots of yelling. After two months of harassment, the week I'd heard so much hype about was now mine to experience firsthand.

The second they opened fire was the last time any of us would be warm and dry for the next five days. The degree of wetness and the intensity of cold would vary, but only enough to stave off hypothermia. Every ounce of food we ate that week would have some amount of sand in it, which actually permanently immunized me from ever being bothered by sand again.

Once we were all soaked, the gate of the cage opened and we scattered like those deer I'd surprised at Muddy Run Park years before. No one had a clue where to go; we just assumed we weren't supposed to stay in the cage. When I think about that moment, it's pretty comical, and I'm sure the instructors got a kick out of seeing a bunch of guys scatter like lost puppies with no idea of what to do next. In the midst of all the gunfire and yelling, we were finally directed to the grinder (the asphalt area inside the fenced BUD/S compound), where the action is best described as a feeding frenzy. Everyone got some "quality time" with an instructor as we began to PT and get thrashed. After all these years, my recollection of my time on the grinder is spotty. However, I do remember the instructors making us run back and forth to the ocean to get wet, each time secretly dragging off a number of my classmates, and then screaming at me to get an accurate headcount.

As if to give us a chance to think about how screwed we were, we were then ordered to get our boats—small rubber rafts known as IBSs (inflatable boat small)—head out beyond the surf zone, and then paddle down the strand to the rock jetty behind the Hotel Del. With much of our time at BUD/S spent in our boats, the class was divided into boat crews of seven men each.

Most evolutions during Hell Week are competitions between boat crews, and it's the time when the SEAL adage of "It pays to be a winner" first plays out. Unlike earlier in our training, when I was concerned with each of my classmates' struggles, during Hell Week, I was concerned only with myself, Rob, and the guys in my boat crew. I expected everyone else to be responsible for himself.

Once down at the jetty, we were ordered to do something known as "night rock portage." The idea was to paddle our IBS in from sea and land on the rocks. It sounds easy, but when the waves are unusually big, as they were for us that night, your boat doesn't land on the rocks so much as it's thrown onto them. Mine was the second boat to make it down to the jetty, but the boat ahead of us just sat beyond the surf zone, so we passed them and headed in for our first landing on the rocks.

In an instant, our boat was thrown completely upside down. As always happens when you have an injury, the part of your body you're trying to protect is the part most likely to get hurt again, and in this case the jagged edge of a rock tore into my right leg, directly into the rope-burn wound I was desperately trying to hide from the instructors.

Although at the time I was too preoccupied with simply surviving to wonder about the point of the exercises, I realized much later the instructors harassed us constantly to assess whether we could think rationally while trying to get through the relentless pounding of the waves, all the while being reminded of how worthless we were. A lack of leadership and teamwork becomes glaringly obvious during moments of chaos. In this case, it took team-wide commitment to a strategy simply to get everyone back into the boat and paddling in the same direction. If the boat crew leader didn't step up fast, someone else typically would. And when that happened, the leader lost all credibility and was naturally relegated to the back. That aspect of SEAL culture was another that I loved. Seniority doesn't matter on the battlefield. What matters is leadership. It's that simple.

Once my boat crew gathered our paddles and climbed into our boat, we headed back out to sea to make another run onto the rocks. Just paddling free of the surf's grip took all our effort and concentration. When we finally made it beyond the surf zone, we paused for a minute, preparing ourselves for another run. It certainly wasn't like being at an amusement park, where you go to the back of the line after your turn on the roller coaster. Many of the boats were in no hurry to go in, so we found ourselves again at the front of the line. With the instructors still screaming from the rocks for someone to come in, we felt obligated to obey. I could tell my leg was bleeding, but I figured I'd have time at some point to check it out. For now, I didn't want to know how bad it was.

So we flowed into our second run in spite of the rough water. This time our landing wasn't much better than the first, but at least no one in our boat got hurt. Once again we chased down our paddles that had been scattered along the shoreline. One of the guys in my boat crew had his paddle snap like a toothpick right below his hands, meaning we now had only six guys paddling. As we were preparing to launch our boat for a third run, we were ordered to stand fast in the surf zone.

I could see the instructors coming together and shouting out to sea, trying to get the other boats to come in. After a few seconds, they fired a flare beyond the surf zone, revealing a number of boats that had not been making their runs. With more than ten boats, it was hard to keep track of which ones were coming in and which weren't. In order to be tracked at night, our kapok lifejackets had chemical lights tied to them, but those who were sitting out the evolution had covered up their lights, thinking they wouldn't be noticed in the darkness.

Everyone was ordered to the beach, where we lined up side by side in the surf zone as the instructors demanded those guilty of not making their runs to reveal themselves. As we were forming up, I took a second to reach down and check out my leg, only to find that the entire lower part of my right pant leg was slimy with blood and seawater. I guessed I'd be spending most of the next five days in the seawater, so infection didn't worry me as much now as it had before. With every bit of my attention on the instructors, I never thought once about being a beacon for sharks.

When no one came clean after a few minutes, we were ordered out of the water and told to strip off our shirts and lifejackets. I'm guessing it was now around 1:30 a.m., so there was no one on the beach or even awake in the hotel to see the show that was about to unfold. Once we all had our shirts off, we were ordered to the edge of the water and told to face the shore, interlock our arms with the guys next to us, and then lie down on our backs in the surf, heads out to sea. This is known as "surf torture." We were going to stay there until ten guys quit.

If you've never thought about the energy in even a one-foot wave, you learn very quickly just how powerful the ocean is, especially when you are defenseless against it. As the waves broke over our faces, we were pushed up the beach over broken seashells, and then dragged back out for another cycle. My shoulders and lower back were taking the brunt of the abuse as I fought to keep my head and face above the water. About the time I began thinking about how much it sucked, we were told to stand up. I noticed a dozen or so guys standing behind the instructors, putting their uniforms back on, but I didn't realize immediately what they were doing.

As the rest of us stood there, already beginning to feel the effects of the cold water, we watched those dozen classmates load up into the back of a pickup truck with their boats and drive off. It had taken less than two hours of Hell Week for almost a fifth of our class to pack it in.

When I reached down to grab my shirt, I finally gave my leg a close look. The sight of it nearly made me vomit. The meat of my shin was torn and swollen from the water. It looked like I had scrambled eggs coming out of my skin. It no longer hurt, but I was scared to death it would become infected and cause me to be pulled out of Hell Week. The only good aspect of the wound was that it was just above my boot and on a part of my leg without a lot of muscle, so my boot didn't rub on it and it was no longer bleeding badly.

By the time the sun rose, we were treading water off a pier on the amphibious base, trying to execute one simple task: count one by one until we had an accurate headcount for our class. Inevitably two or more guys would yell out the next number simultaneously and we'd have to start all over. Just moments before, we had finished doing back flutter kicks while lying naked on the steel pier adjacent to where we were now treading water—still naked. That was another time we were ordered to do something until at least ten guys packed it in. So now, with another ten guys gone and having been cold and wet for about six hours, we were growing increasingly impatient to get an accurate headcount so we could get the hell out of the fifty-six-degree water. Before we even got close to finishing, another group of guys swam to a ladder extending down from the steel pier and climbed out. They, too, had decided they'd had enough. Finally, with another group of guys gone, we disciplined ourselves enough to complete the count. We climbed out of the water, put our uniforms back on, put our boats on our heads, and ran off to the chow hall for our first meal of Hell Week.

I wish I'd had the wherewithal to notice the looks we most certainly were getting from everyone in the mess hall. I'm sure we already appeared shell-shocked and beaten down, but I only remember sitting at my table, chewing my eggs about a thousand times per bite just to get them down without throwing them back up. Rob and I never did get a chance to talk during that week, since we were in different boat crews, but he would tell me later that when we ate, he found it depressing to think about having to end his brief enjoyment of a hot meal—knowing his boat (which we carried on our heads or paddled everywhere that week) was waiting outside for his return. By midweek Rob was regularly falling asleep as he waited in line for chow. I imagine the warmth of the dining hall was all it took to knock him unconscious. His body would fortunately give one last convulsion, waking him up and keeping him from hitting the deck.

For me, Hell Week was similar to running a race, where the initial part is so tough you wonder what you were thinking to subject yourself to the discomfort, but once you settle into a rhythm, you remember why you do it. So once I got through the first night, it actually got a lot easier. More importantly, Hell Week was a time for everyone to find out on his own who he was. For me, this week was something I'd been building up to for a long time, and it was going to affirm the influence of my upbringing in a big way.

Following breakfast, that Monday was filled with constant motion. We ran, we swam, we negotiated the obstacle course, and we were in the water *a lot*. As sunset approached on that first full day, we found ourselves in Coronado Bay to complete something akin to a waterborne obstacle course without our boats but with our paddles, which made swimming tougher.

Another BUD/S adage is "You're only as fast as the slowest swimmer." This becomes painfully apparent during Hell Week, when you have to stay together as a boat crew while executing every evolution. There was one exceptional swimmer on our team who had the biggest calf muscles I'd ever seen, and though our crew finished second or third in most races, I knew he had to be frustrated with the rest of us for being so comparatively slow. We'd been assigned to boat crews according to height, and the "short guy" boat crew kicked ass and finished first every time by a wide margin, getting to relax during the time it took for the rest of us "fenderheads" (a term of endearment used by our proctor, referring to big rubber bumpers placed between ships to prevent contact with the pier or another ship) to finish. They didn't get to sleep, but at least they didn't get thrashed while they waited.

By the time we all finished the waterborne obstacle course we were seriously jack-hammering. "Jack-hammering" is the term we used to describe the uncontrollable shaking of our bodies because of the cold. As we stood next to our boats with paddles in hand, the instructors told us that because all but one boat crew seemed to be trying, we were going to get back in the water to have another shot at giving it a better effort. I could hear the class collectively groan. I whispered as quietly as I could to my boat crew to stand fast because I knew, or rather I *hoped*, they couldn't be serious. I had barely gotten the words out of my mouth when I heard the sound of paddles hitting the ground. Another group of guys had had enough and were done. They, too, loaded into the back of the pickup truck that was now idling in front of us. Just before they drove off, one of the instructors told us to wave goodbye to them, then announced that we wouldn't be getting back into the water, at least not right then.

Not even twenty-four hours into the week, dozens had dropped out, and those of us who remained were zombie-like from the crazed pace we'd been maintaining. The cold, more than anything else, was taking its toll on the class. But, while I hated the cold as much as ever, so far it wasn't nearly as unbearable as the cold I had experienced while hunting with my father. At least now I could tell I had fingers and toes. If someone had told me years before, when Dad walked me back to the truck because I was nearly frozen, that I would benefit from all those hours freezing my young ass off, I would have told them they were nuts. But there I was, miserable, but not even close to the limit of what I knew I could endure.

As odd as it may sound, the daylight hours during Hell Week are a blur, but I remember the nights in amazing detail, even though Hell Week was more than thirty years ago. The first full night was a continuation of the day's events. I remember going to the swimming pool on the amphibious base and racing as boat crews against one another. Perhaps to further expose us to the elements, we were again instructed to strip out of our uniforms completely. Who knows, maybe my memory has been distorted by time and we were actually given wetsuits to wear, but I'm willing to bet we were naked, because I remember sitting "nuts to butt" with my arms wrapped around the guy in front of me, trying desperately to keep from freezing to death. In our seven-man boat crews, we must have looked like fourteen-legged freak shows sitting next to the pool, snuggling and jack-hammering, trying to find just a little warmth. I heard someone in the lane next to mine begging someone in his crew to urinate so he'd feel something warm. I told my guys that I was nowhere near cold enough for that and to save their relief for when they got back in the water. My plea went unheeded, but at least it made us laugh momentarily as, one by one, we felt the flow of something warm on our asses.

In an effort to push us to our physical and mental limits, we spent extended periods of time in the water, especially during those first few days. The days seemed more focused on beating us down physically, while nights were spent on cognitive function drills designed to keep us moving and thinking. The most dangerous events took place early in the week while we were still somewhat alert and coordinated.

One afternoon early in the week we paddled to another beach and played "games" in the mud off and on until sunset. In between the games we collected driftwood, which we passed off to our instructors, who crafted it into a huge pile to be burned later for a bonfire.

After sunset, we were ordered to disperse from the campsite we had spent the afternoon constructing for an event known as "stealth and concealment." The idea was for each of us individually, not as a boat crew, to attempt to make it back to the camp perimeter without being discovered by an instructor. Some of my classmates were quite skilled at concealment and gave the task their full effort, but not me. Sneaking up on a deer was one thing, but the idea that I could possibly sneak up on trained killers undetected was crazy talk. So, once I reached a position out of sight from the campsite, I simply started belly-crawling toward the campsite, totally unconcerned that I would be discovered. The entire time I was crawling back to the campsite, not a single instructor passed anywhere near me; in fact, I never saw any of them looking for us. When I finally got within fifteen yards of the campsite, I could make out all the instructors sitting around the beautiful bonfire we'd made for them, just bullshitting. I thought to myself, *This is Grampa and Marion all over again, sitting in the boat, forgetting they were supposed try to find me.* I continued crawling toward the campsite and got within a few yards when one of the instructors said, "Come on in, Eschbach."

Because we could not wear watches during Hell Week, trying to recall time is impossible, but I'm assuming it took about an hour for the entire class to make it to the campsite. As we waited for the others, those of us already inside the perimeter were allowed to lie within range of the bonfire. Again, most of us lay spooning (although this time fully clothed) with whomever was next to us, trying to get warmer. Fortunately for me, Rob was already there, so I chose my good friend to nuzzle up next to. I'm sure that sounds odd, but when you're as cold as we were, you'll do almost anything to find some warmth.

The moments next to that fire are the only ones I recall from that week when I was in a fair amount of physical discomfort. My hips were cramping up in a big way and I was unable to find any relief from the pain as I lay in that spooning position. I finally decided to give up siphoning off Rob's warmth and stood up to stretch for a while.

Once the class was accounted for, we began our next event, something called "Life Stories," during which, one by one, when called on by an instructor, we'd each tell our life's story. After one classmate told his story, the next guy chosen would have to repeat it before telling his own. Failure to accurately recount the story to the satisfaction of the instructors led to some minor thrashing before we could move on.

One of my classmates spent some of his story time recounting his summertime employment at an Anheuser-Busch beer distributor in the Midwest. That was all fine until the dumbass decided to recite the entire Anheuser-Busch brewing process description printed on every can and bottle of Budweiser:

"This is the famous Budweiser beer. We know of no brand produced by any other brewer which costs so much to brew and age. Our exclusive beechwood aging produces a taste, a smoothness, and a drinkability you will find in no other beer at any price. Brewed by our original all-natural process using the choicest hops, rice and best barley malt."

Son-of-a-bitch if he didn't know the damn thing word for word, even tired out of his mind. I guess that was the point of the exercise.

The instructors seemed to know instantly who was going to have to recount this guy's story, and sure enough it was me. I knew I didn't stand a chance, so, rather than waiting to be informed of my punishment, I simply jumped to my feet, ran like hell to the water, dove in, and then rolled around in the sand until I was the perfect "sugar cookie" (the punishment of choice for most of our early training). Once back at the bonfire it was my turn to tell my life's story. As best as I can recall, all I said was, "I was born in Pennsylvania, I once was the best damn slow dancer at the Mifflinburg VFW, and I'm in Class 124." That was it. My favorite instructor, who would take my boat crew on most of our long night adventures that week, looked at me and said, "Well done, Eschbach."

The last three days of Hell Week all seemed to run together. Like I said, the nights were just a series of long races around Coronado, and aside from one event I'll describe later, it wasn't too bad. I was able to hide the severity of my leg injury until the first of our two medical checkups. The checkups occurred at night, out in the open wherever our escapades had taken us. We'd be ordered to strip down naked and form a line, one behind the other, in front of the corpsman doing our inspection. He gave every inch of our bodies a good look or touch.

When it was my turn, the corpsman began at my head and worked his way down my body until he saw the wound on my leg. Knowing what was ahead of us, he told me he should really pull me out because there was a good chance my leg would become infected. I felt my eyes well up instantly, and I quietly begged him to let me proceed with my class. This corpsman was one of our first-phase instructors, and someone I really enjoyed. It didn't take much pleading before he told me to put my uniform back on and not to let him see the wound again before the end of Hell Week.

After more than 200 miles of running and swimming, with virtually no sleep, the week finally came to a close with us down the strand at the demolition pit on Friday morning for one last round of harassment. It almost seemed like a victory lap, as we all sensed the onslaught was about to officially end. The instructors stood around the edge of the slime- and mud-filled pit, throwing us sandwiches and apples from boxed lunches. We crawled out of the demolition pit and carried our boats to the surf zone for one last paddle, this time back to the BUD/S compound where the week had begun five days earlier. The instructors had told us to form up along the shoreline with our boats to await their decision as to whether we had performed well enough to secure from Hell Week. After a few minutes of standing there shoulder-to-shoulder with the few of us who remained, the heads of our instructors began to emerge above the sand dune and into view in front of us. I have no idea what they said, I just remember standing at the end of the line next to the class leading petty officer, who said to me, "I think I'm gonna cry."

One by one, the instructors made their way down the line,

shaking our hands. I was the last guy acknowledged. The sensation is impossible to describe, so I will just say it was probably the greatest feeling of accomplishment I have ever known. I didn't know it at that moment, but for the rest of my life, I would compare every hard day at sea or in my personal life to that week. Just as my circumstances would always be compared to that farmer with one arm, now everything I considered tough would be compared to Hell Week.

All those hours spent in the water with my grandfather, those torturous cross-country practices, that summer on the farm, and the miserably cold days hunting with Dad had really prepared me for Hell Week. That doesn't mean that it wasn't challenging, or something I'd want to do again, but my perspective on life, and my attitude of not being entitled to anything, allowed me to go through Hell Week accepting, without question, everything we were made to do.

In groups of eight to ten, we loaded into the backs of pickup trucks and were taken to the amphibious base to be checked out physically before being released for the weekend. It was the first time in five days that Rob and I got to talk to one another. As it turned out, Rob had completed Hell Week with a full-blown case of bronchitis and was dangerously close to developing pneumonia. Typical Rob, he never brought attention to how he was feeling. The only thing I remember from that checkup was how quickly my feet swelled up after taking my boots off, since they had been on all week with the exception of the times we were naked. I recall looking at my feet and thinking they had to belong to someone at least three hundred pounds heavier.

∞

The Monday after Hell Week was somewhat surreal. It was hard to believe that the week we had been waiting for was over and we had made it through. My leg was still raw, but it wasn't getting any worse. The only lingering effect of the week for most of us was the poor conditions of our feet. Because of this, we had been instructed to show up that Monday in sneakers, which really took the wind out of our sails. At least it did mine. It's hard to feel like a badass when you're wearing sneakers.

We had been told to form up on the obstacle course first thing on Monday. I couldn't imagine that we would be running the course so soon after Hell Week, but we showed up there as ordered. Waiting for us by the start of the course was one of my favorite instructors. He had been wounded multiple times in Vietnam and was the one instructor who never went out of his way to abuse us. He was one of those men who didn't say more than needed to be said, and what he did say always held meaning.

But today there was something odd in his demeanor. I fully expected to be welcomed on that first day after Hell Week as if we had finally accomplished something significant, but the reception was anything but that. I had no sooner presented the class than he began verbally tearing us down and reminding us that we hadn't done shit. He ordered us onto the obstacle course to retrieve the telephone poles that made up one of the obstacles known as the Belly Robber, and which are used for "log PT." Log PT is a workout that is executed as a boat crew, meaning the seven guys assigned to a boat do various exercises as a team using the log as weight. You do overhead presses, bench presses, sit-ups with the log lying across your waist, and whatever else the instructor demands. Log PT sucks. It's an exercise where everyone feels like they are the only one lifting the log, with the rest of the team barely putting out any effort.

As we always did, the first thing we had to do was to take our logs into the surf zone to get them, as well as ourselves, wet. We then had to make our logs, and ourselves, into sugar cookies before we could race back to the instructor and begin doing our PT. Just as my boat crew cleared the dune and raced toward the instructor, I heard a dull pop behind me. It wasn't loud, just different. Then one of my classmates dropped to the ground and began screaming in pain. Perhaps from the stress of Hell Week, his shinbone couldn't handle the weight of the log. His lower leg had snapped.

That ended the log PT session and we were ordered back to the compound to meet with our proctor. By now, the mood had changed. Our proctor welcomed us to the rest of first phase. I remember him saying that he was certain each of us had considered quitting at least once during Hell Week, but I shook my head no, because that thought had never entered my mind—not even for a second.

The last month of first phase was actually a lot of fun. Our instructors seemed to really enjoy messing with us. One example that typifies their antics occurred during our underwater knot-tying practical. I recall it being after Hell Week because there were only a few of us in the class, and with the limited space around the inside of the dive tower, there was no way we could have gotten the entire pre-Hell Week class up there. As I said earlier, every new evolution had to be demonstrated for the class, and because the instructors had long ago done the exercises themselves, it was up to me to show everyone how to complete the task. Even though I had never done it before either, as the class leader I was expected to learn on the fly. I would always listen intently to the instructions and then execute as told without asking any questions. I knew that if I did ask a question, the answer would be something I didn't want to hear, so I just did what I thought I heard.

The instructions for the underwater knot tying went as follows. "Eschbach, you'll get in the water, and when ready, you'll dive down to eighteen feet where you'll meet an instructor next to a cable stretching across the dive tank. Immediately tie your first knot around the cable. Once given the thumbs-up, you'll untie that knot and proceed to the next knot until you have successfully completed tying the first four knots. After that you'll resume your dive down to fifty feet where another instructor will be waiting for you. Once on the bottom, you'll tie your final knot. Upon receiving the thumbs-up, you'll come back to the surface, having successfully completed the practical. Any questions?"

You could almost hear all of us thinking, *You must be out of your mind. Only one breath?* But none of us dared ask whether we were allowed a second breath. As always, I wasn't about to say a word other than "I got it."

I jumped into the water, secured my facemask, grasped my rope, and took one big breath before heading down eighteen feet to the first stop of the descent. I was glad to see my favorite instructor at that first stop, as I had a feeling that even if I messed up one of the four knots, he'd give me the thumbs-up anyway. But I breezed through the first four knots, threw one hand over my head, squeezed my nose with the other hand, and drifted down to fifty feet.

As I neared the bottom of the dive tank, and with about five more feet of descent to go, I could no longer equalize the pressure in my ears. I'd been dealing with a minor head cold that week and like every other ache or pain I had while there, I stayed as far away from medical as I could in order to ensure I wouldn't be sidelined or even rolled back to another class. Rather than head to the surface, I restarted my descent and pushed myself to the bottom. As I stood on the bottom about to begin my final knot I could hear my ears hissing as the pressure equalized.

The final knot was a square knot—something that's pretty tough to mess up. But waiting for me at the bottom was the one instructor I knew didn't like me. It seemed at every opportunity he singled me out for either a verbal belittling, or some individual physical harassment. I sensed he didn't agree with some of the other instructors who seemed to like me, and believed I'd done nothing to earn even the slightest relief from the training. Whatever his reasons, seeing him on the bottom and knowing he was all that stood between me and the surface of the dive tower was demoralizing. As I approached my limit of how long I could hold my breath, he proceeded to give each of my first three, perfect attempts at a square knot a thumbs down. Finally, after my fourth attempt, he gave the okay and I shot to the surface as fast as I could. As soon as I broke the surface I could see the looks on my classmates' faces. They seemed to say, *How in the heck did you do that?* My proctor and the other instructors just laughed their asses off as my proctor said, "Alan, did I forget to tell you to come to the surface for another breath after your first four knots?"

∞

Although finishing Hell Week was a significant accomplishment, it was a month or so later in my training that I received a compliment that meant even more to me. Because I always felt that if I could do something, anyone could, I never consciously compared myself to anyone else. Where I stood in the class was irrelevant to me as long as I knew I gave every task my best effort. Likewise, I didn't spend a lot of time worrying what my instructors' opinions of me were; nonetheless, I valued their opinions because of the respect I had for them.

In any event, one morning we were out beyond the surf zone when someone started blowing the horn of the medical truck. At BUD/S we always had some form of medical assistance standing by in case something went wrong. We also had to learn semaphore during first phase so the instructors could communicate with us by waving flags while we were far offshore beyond the range of their voices. For this particular evolution, I was paired with a classmate I'll call Harmony. Because some of the guys (including Harmony) had forgotten semaphore by this point, I told him to write down the letters on the Plexiglas we carried with us as I identified them. One by one, I spoke the letters until they spelled "ESCHBACH, GET THE FUCK IN HERE." Harmony and I swam ashore. There, I was met by my first-phase proctor, who ushered me into the front seat of the medical truck where another of my earlier phase instructors, whom I had barely seen over the past month, was waiting for me. Without fanfare, this instructor told me that he was about to transfer and wanted me to know before he detached that I was the best officer he had seen in his three years at BUD/S.

I was speechless, and quite honestly, I almost teared up. Hearing those words came as a relief, and for the first time in three months I felt as if I had accomplished everything I had come to BUD/S to accomplish. It's almost unfathomable to think that those words of praise served not as motivation to go forward, but rather as a catalyst for what I did next.

Surviving the daily onslaught of abuse and being told I was worthless all those weeks had subconsciously kept me focused and given me a reason to keep trying. As I said, being a SEAL wasn't what intrigued me; rather it was a desire to know if I could handle the training. Now, finally getting the affirmation I thought I wanted did nothing but leave me doubting why I was there. As I sat in my room later that evening, those words continued their assault on my focus. It was a strange realization, almost an epiphany, now understanding why some coaches or teachers I had in the past never offered their unqualified approval. They knew the potential impact it could have on someone's determination and effort. Until that moment, I would have never imagined being susceptible to that style of leadership. Perhaps that's the one pitfall of not having dreams.

Beyond this new sense of doubt, there were more concrete concerns. One aspect of SEAL life in particular made me begin to reconsider that career choice. By the time second phase started, I'd started to wrestle mentally and emotionally with how I would be able to reconcile the demands of the SEAL lifestyle with my desire to have a family. During the last month of first phase, with Hell Week behind us, the instructors were more open to discussing the realities of those demands. I knew from discussions with my instructors that as a SEAL, even when I wasn't deployed, I would be all over the map for training. It began to weigh on me that if I did have children, I would likely spend very little time with them.

I phoned my wife and told her I was considering dropping out because I wanted us to start a family. That was the moment I realized her reasons for marrying me were quite different from mine for marrying her. She told me that if I quit, she would be leaving me because she refused to live with a quitter. I had hoped she would allay my concerns by offering her support and acknowledging that having a family was a priority for her, but that wasn't the case.

I spent the next few weeks struggling with what to do. It was amazing how those thoughts affected my physical performance. For the first three months, I had done well on every run, been in the upper quarter of the class on the obstacle course, and had consistently been the number two or three swimming pair in my class. There had never been any physical challenge that I didn't successfully complete on my first attempt. My instructors liked me. I loved my classmates and had made a great friend in Rob, and I was enjoying training because we were no longer being constantly harassed. My mind had been completely clear of any outside distractions.

Yet now, as I started to realize the contrast between my personal desires and my professional priorities, my performance began to spiral downward. Every physical challenge became a struggle for me. Even runs, which had once been a relative breeze, became a grind. I was finishing almost last in my class. Making things even worse, I now had to deal with the reality that my four-month marriage was likely going to end—something I didn't want to be true.

My classmates, especially Rob, could tell that something was wrong with me. Looking back, I know what I needed was a swift kick in the ass, but I doubt anyone felt comfortable giving it to me. I phoned the Surface Warfare detailer and asked what my options would be if I quit. When he told me he could only offer me a ship in Coronado, I decided to just stay put, spend two years as a SEAL, and then go back to the surface community. A few weeks after that one and only call to my detailer, he phoned and informed me that if I was still considering leaving, he could place me on a new Aegis-Class cruiser that would be home ported in Norfolk, Virginia. I hung up the phone, went to see my proctor, and quit.

I knew instantly I had done the wrong thing when I rang that bell. But there was no taking it back. That was a time before I knew that if you weren't happy with how you spent your professional life, no amount of joy in your personal life could make up for that or offset it. I guess it was the first of those things I wish my father had revealed to me somewhere along the way.

From that moment until I sat down to write this book, I managed to avoid wondering "What if?" I knew if I dwelled on what I had given up and what I had done to my classmates, it would have kept me from ever moving forward. I hated that I put my personal desires ahead of my classmates', and regretted not realizing how much they liked me and depended on my leadership. I hated knowing also that in every sense of the word, I quit. I should have relied on the perspective of my upbringing that had served me so well in life up to that point to pull me through that situation. But I didn't. I've learned from that experience and sadly others since then that getting out of my own head is often my biggest obstacle.

As close as Rob and I had become, and as much as I loved my classmates, I never tried to keep in touch. My severance was clean. In my mind, I had forever given up the privilege and right to talk with them and share laughs about our time at BUD/S. In the years that followed, some of the guys, including Rob, did reach out to me, and we were able to pick back up like old friends do. Those gestures of friendship and understanding mean more than I can express.

Even with the way I ended my time there, I was now more at peace with who I was than ever before. That experience of doing so well under challenging conditions gave me the confidence to believe that no matter how outside the norm I might see things, my view still had some validity. It clarified and ultimately solidified my understanding of who I was as a person, and it gave me a confidence in who I was that I had never known before.

It took years for me to realize all I had learned when I was there. I learned much about myself, as well as a lot regarding the inherent human fears and tendencies that nearly all men share. What I found was that everyone has some amount of apprehension about something in his or her life. I learned that when I gave something my best effort, it typically turned out pretty well. And I learned that true courage is about acknowledging and overcoming your fears. I also realized that in any situation, there will always be someone who is more uncomfortable than I, and although it doesn't sound like something to be proud of, I found some real motivation in that. Going back to the fleet after experiencing those last four months at BUD/S made my courage to stand by my beliefs, no matter the risk or the consequences, even stronger than before.

My wife and I did the best we could to stay together, but after six years, we divorced. Neither of us ever blamed the other. It was just a matter of us wanting and needing different things. She had some wonderful qualities, and those are the only ones I care to remember.

PHOTOGRAPHS

Hitching shelter in Quarryville, Pennsylvania

Eddie (age 3) and me (age 5), November 1963

Me, Dad, and Eddie on opening day of squirrel season 1972

Grampa (right) in Myitkyina, Burma,
field hospital 1944

Me and my Aunt Dawna just prior to reporting to BUD/S

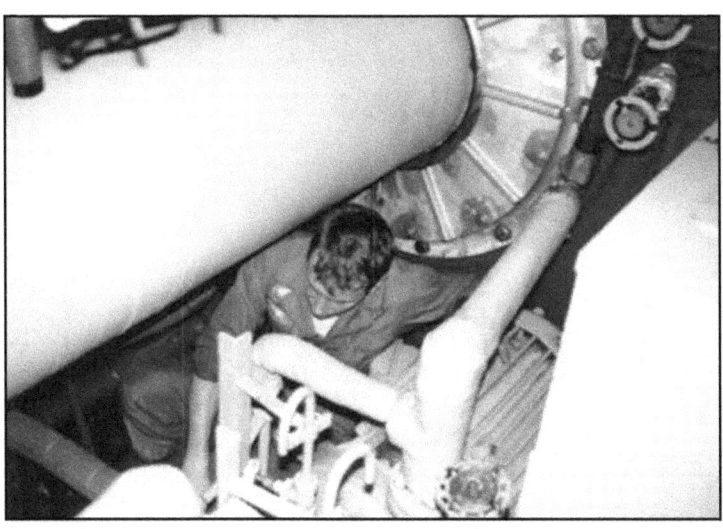

Back at the site of the fuel oil leak on the USS *Thomas S. Gates* after a shower and clean coveralls

Mike and me on the flight deck of USS *Thomas S. Gates*

Me and my Executive Officer John Dorey on the bridge wing during a refueling with USNS *Pecos*

My strike group commander, Rear Admiral McArthur, and me after my final remarks as USS *Arleigh Burke*'s commanding officer

USS *Arleigh Burke* (DDG-51), the lead ship of the *Arleigh Burke*-class guided missile destroyers

A page from my journal

Part Three

The Road from BUD/S to Command at Sea

"People don't care how much you know until they know how much you care."

—Theodore Roosevelt

CHAPTER TWELVE

USS *Thomas S. Gates*

By the time I reached my department head tour in the spring of 1989, all of my earlier years' insecurities and doubts were gone. Having completed another ship tour, as well as my first shore duty assignment, I reported aboard USS *Thomas S. Gates* at peace with who I was and completely unconcerned with anything beyond my department and supporting the eighty or so men whom I had been given the privilege to lead. Rather than being in the place so many find themselves—where they love where they've been, hate where they are, and can't wait to get to where they are going—I couldn't have been more satisfied with where I was in life at that moment. If ever I had reached nirvana, this was it.

However, while I had reached that comfortable place in my personal life, the thirty months that followed were going to be filled with tests and experiences that would come to serve me well in my professional life some ten years later. The relationships I formed with my men, my division officers, and my fellow officers became the most rewarding of my career to that point, and further validated that my focus on taking care of my people above all else was ultimately all that really mattered.

As the engineer officer on *Thomas S. Gates*, my equipment responsibilities spanned from stem to stern. My men possessed skill sets that covered all the engineering and damage control specialties on board. Hardworking, smart, tireless, humble, and incredibly dedicated and loyal, they were the finest group of men I had worked with since my classmates at BUD/S.

My predecessor was collegial and gracious during the turnover, and he delivered to me a department that had no issues to speak of. I couldn't have walked into a better situation. The captain and the wardroom welcomed and accepted me into their midst without hesitation.

My first priority, aside from gaining an advanced knowledge of my equipment, was to individually assess and get to know and understand each man in my department. Because I had come to appreciate the influence of my perspective on life, I recognized the value in understanding the perspectives of the eighty men in my department. I was certain that every achievement or success of our department would be traced back to positive, caring leadership.

Unlike those instructors I'd known during division officer school, it was important to me that I was liked, and I couldn't have cared less what anyone thought of that. When people like you enough that the last thing they want to do is disappoint you, they try even harder to succeed. Taking the time to get to know someone not only serves the purpose of understanding their perspective, but also begins to show them that you care about something beyond just the mission or yourself. Perhaps the biggest reason I wanted to get to know my guys and for them to know me was because I knew how much *I* was going to need *them*.

In my experience, the most challenging naval job is that of department head. In that position you are expected to be the expert in your field. Major decisions critical to the success of the ship depend on your advice and your assessment of what needs to be done for every aspect of your responsibilities. As the engineering department head on *Gates*, I knew there would be long, challenging days, and I knew the best way to stay energized would be to interact with my guys, so that's exactly what I did.

Many times I would find myself sitting in my stateroom feeling overwhelmed with all I had to do, and whenever unease started to take root, I would get up and walk down to my spaces simply to spend time with my guys. In every case it instantly brightened and lightened my mood.

While on the *Gates* I worked for three superb commanding officers. Each was quite different from the others, but all were professional and smart and loved being captain. It was during this tour that I first began to realize the incredible privilege it is to have people who are yours to look after and care for, and how positive leadership from the top can make even the most challenging times ones you will always cherish.

Within the first twenty-two months of my tour, *Gates* completed a standard six-month Mediterranean cruise, a nearly eight-month cruise to the Middle East (when we left with only ninety-six hours notice in response to Iraq's invasion of Kuwait), and two two-month counternarcotics operations. Spending roughly eighteen of twenty-two months away from homeport was quite possibly the best period of my life. I remember so many times during that tour looking at my captain, my roommate, or my guys and fellow department heads, and thinking to myself that there was no place on Earth I'd rather be.

I remarried about a year into my tour on *Gates*. During the first year of my marriage, I saw my wife less than two months and came home from that second deployment with a three-month-old daughter I had never seen. I remember sitting in the engineering control station on the morning we returned from that eight-month cruise and saying to my senior chief gas turbine specialist, Mike Meeink, that I wasn't ready to go topside. I had come to rely so heavily on the guys in my department that I wasn't ready to say goodbye to them or that cruise. Even if it was to see my daughter for the first time, I knew my life very likely would never be better than it had been for those eight months. Even now I can't say for sure that those feelings aren't still true on some level.

It was during this tour when I began to appreciate how special it was to be deployed over the holidays, because I felt like my being deployed allowed someone else to be home. I loved being in the company of my friends and shipmates, seeing them spend time away from their families over the holidays and remain upbeat. It is a feeling that is impossible to express adequately.

I was further blessed during that tour to work with some amazingly talented fellow department heads. The department head tour represents the most important in a Surface Warfare officer's career. It is the tour on which all emphasis for selection to command at sea is placed. Most U.S. Navy warships are comprised of six departments: engineering, operations, combat systems, weapons, supply, and navigation and administration. Competition between the department heads is often inherently spirited and stressful. It is especially difficult and challenging when the department heads don't support one another. However, on *Gates* my fellow department heads became and remain some of my closest friends. Nevin Carr, Eric Sweigard, Steve Hampton, and Pat Piercey were the perfect guys with whom to share the experience. Each was smart, witty, and most importantly, completely unselfish and committed to working for the benefit of the ship.

After about six months on board, my situation got even better when the last of my "inherited" division officers detached, leaving me with a department of all ensign division officers and just one second-tour officer. I know it may not sound like a good thing to have such inexperienced officers running my divisions, but I loved the opportunity to help guide them during this critical tour in their young careers. Fortunately for me, they were all unbelievably talented and hard-working young officers. I still have the utmost respect for each of them, and those who have remained in the navy have all advanced to major command and beyond.

Rounding out the incredible hand I was dealt was my roommate. As a department head, I typically had a room to myself unless we were underway for an extended period and embarked a helicopter detachment. In those instances, one of the pilots, normally the squadron maintenance officer, would room with me. Because *Gates* spent so much time underway, and because we normally embarked the same helicopter squadron, my roommate and I quickly became close friends.

His name was Mike Pohlkamp, and he was simply one of those people so special, it defies articulation, though I'll try. Mike was easily the funniest guy I had ever met. In addition, he had a personality and engaging confidence that everyone in the wardroom loved. Guys would come into our stateroom every day after dinner to participate in some of the daily "games" we played, or to flip through his photo album from his time at the University of Missouri.

On days when I'd find myself tired or mired down in the routine, Mike would have something to say or do that would pull me out of it. One of the things he did that became an almost daily routine would occur as I entered our room. Mike would say, "Hello, Eschbaugh," emphasizing the "baugh."

I would say, "It's Esch*bach*. Like the composer."

To which Mike would reply in an elevated tone, "'Ey, I changed it," followed immediately by his favorite expression, "You heard me!" Then we'd laugh and talk or play "full-court" basketball in our small stateroom. I enjoyed our friendship greatly, and I knew that like most things in life, those days of rooming together would end all too soon. It was the same awareness of the special things in life that I first experienced as a kid on that trout stream, and I am so thankful I took the time to appreciate my time with Mike while it was happening.

A few months after our return from deployment, we were back at sea, heading south to Puerto Rico. It was sometime around one o'clock in the morning when our general alarm was sounded, setting a condition known as General Quarters. General Quarters sends the entire crew to their battle stations, and it's from this condition that the ship is best prepared to fight, as well as counter battle damage. So General Quarters is set during conditions of combat, as well as when the ship encounters internal fires or flooding.

On this night, General Quarters was set in response to a major fuel oil leak in one of our two main engine rooms. On most ships, the engineer officer reports immediately to the central engineering control station and oversees the ship's damage control teams. From there, he or she keeps the captain apprised of the situation and makes recommendations for how to battle the casualty.

As the engineer officer on *Gates*, I found it difficult to go to the central control station without first going to the scene of the flood or fire. Standard procedure on most ships would have been for my men to go the scene first while I sat safely in the central control station—but that didn't feel right to me. It felt cowardly. So shortly after reporting to *Gates*, I approached my captain and told him I'd be going directly to the scene of any casualties we sustained because it would allow me to get a situation report to him more quickly, and because I'd have a better understanding of what my guys were heading into.

On this night when we sounded our alarm and announced it was for a major fuel oil leak in one of our main engineering spaces, I ran directly to the scene. When I opened the door, I was shocked by the density of the fuel vapors that had already spread through the space, leaving every surface slick with fuel. As I raced down the first ladder to the upper level, my foot slipped on a rung and I fell onto the deck grating above the reduction gear.

Pulling myself to my feet, I made it down the next two ladders to the bilge level, where I found my two watch standers searching desperately for the source of the leak. What I could see was a geyser spraying up out of the bilge, sending fuel in every direction. My guys were shutting every value in the fuel oil system, but to no effect.

By then my senior chief engineman, Tom Fitzgerald, was on the lower level with us. I had met Tom years before while going through advanced fire-fighting school, and had asked him to be part of my two-man team (me and him) because he was strong, knowledgeable on damage control, fearless, and pretty damn funny. I figured that if I was going to die responding to something like this, he'd at least be sure to make me laugh once we knew all was lost.

Finding the source of the leak was proving to be impossible. I had one of the watch standers call the central control station and order them not to send anyone else into the space until we could isolate the leak. As one of my guys entered the bilge from the lower level, I went up one deck and crawled back down into the bilge through a hatch under the exhaust trunk of our generator. Once back in the bilge, I continued crawling along, moving my hands back and forth in front of me, trying to find the leak.

By now, all four of us in the space were covered in fuel. If a fire broke out, which was a real possibility, we all would have died or been severely burned. As I inched my way farther under the deck grating toward the leak, I heard one of my guys yell, "Class Charlie fire!" That meant we now had an electrical fire to deal with. I was certain it was a matter of seconds before flames erupted and consumed the space.

Even with a major fire now a very real possibility, not a soul left their station. Everyone stood fast and continued frantically trying to find the source of the leak, or to protect the two of us in the bilge.

What we didn't know was that the "fire" was a false alarm. One of my watch standers had accidently sprayed our firefighting agent on the motor controller for the lube oil purifier heater, causing the motor controller to arc. When smoke was seen coming through the vents of the control box, my watch stander assumed there was a fire. Fortunately for us, the box didn't ignite.

Finally, one of my guys and I simultaneously found a split in the top of one our fuel tanks. That's why there was no way to isolate the leak. The fuel would continue to spray out of the tank's top until we could plug the four-inch split. I pushed four of my fingers into the crack while the young man in the bilge with me used a hacksaw to cut off a drain line that was directly above the ruptured area. Senior Chief Fitzgerald took a wooden wedge and some oakum and drove it into the split.

Over the next few hours, we pumped the fuel out of the space, ventilated the area, and used a chemical bond to seal the crack. We then transferred the remaining fuel in the tank to other storage tanks to prevent another fuel leak should our patch fail.

After the leak repairs were wrapped up, I thanked the watch standers for their courage and expressed my admiration for how they never once considered leaving the space. I can remember looking at each of them, their coveralls drenched with fuel, thinking how calm they all appeared. None of them seemed shaken by how close we had all come to a more serious outcome. I loved being surrounded by sailors who worked hard, but never made that hard work look unpleasant. They were a special group.

∽

As wonderful as the people were, my tour on *Gates* did come with some leadership challenges. The biggest occurred roughly twenty-seven months into my tour. In addition to having been gone nearly seventy-five percent of that time, we had completed two Operational Propulsion Plant Exams (which tested every aspect of engineering and damage control material readiness), as well as a comprehensive, ship-wide inspection known as INSURV. In all three inspections, engineering and damage control performed far above fleet average, and in fact were assessed to be "virtually flawless" during the INSURV, which was considered an unparalleled accomplishment at that time.

Shortly after our INSURV inspection, the second of my three commanding officers during that tour detached and was replaced by the last one I would serve under while on *Gates*. Unlike the first two, who had been exceptional athletes at the Naval Academy and professionally playful and relaxed, my third commanding officer held a master's degree in physics as well as an undergraduate physics degree from the College of William and Mary. I don't know if it paints the proper picture of him to say he was the intellectual type, but compared to my first two captains, he certainly came across that way.

As in any work environment, the arrival of a new boss, especially a ship's new captain, can be a tough transition for a number of reasons. When the new boss takes over from a man as confident and universally well liked as my second captain, it's especially difficult.

As a department head approaching the final six months of such a uniquely busy and successful tour, all I wanted to do was gain my new commanding officer's respect and detach unscathed. But, two days after the change of command, the ship got underway for another two-month counternarcotics operation, and, as always seems to happen when there is a new commanding officer, the engineering plant suffered some unusual casualties that had me briefing my new boss about a dozen times a day. Most sailors believe that when there's someone new in charge, the ship knows it and acts up in a number of unusual, if not mysterious, ways. That's exactly what happened in my department.

My first real glimpse into my new captain's personality came after my fifth or sixth visit to his cabin during that first underway. After giving him more bad news, I turned to walk out of his cabin when he stopped me and said, "Alan, don't waste your time worrying about whether you're going to be as smart as me. I've been first in my class at every level of my education, so I doubt you're smarter than I am."

That might sound conceited, but it actually struck me as a rather thoughtful thing for him to say. He was clearly trying to make me feel better about all the problems we were having with the engineering plant. I wasn't the least bit offended by his comment because by that point in my life and in that tour, I was damn sure there were lots of people smarter than me. He just happened to be the latest in a long line of those people.

In the midst of all the equipment casualties, the new captain would walk around the ship every day, making notes for each department head and pointing out deficiencies in our departments that he wanted us to address. I received these notes for a few days before going to see him to make sure he knew that, although I wasn't ignoring his input, the fact that the notes were from him didn't automatically put his observations at the top of my list. I told him where they fit into my departmental priorities, giving him the opportunity to "recalibrate" my priorities if he disagreed. Not knowing him well at all at that point, I couldn't get a read on what he thought of that, but I decided not to worry about it. Considering what was about to happen a few months later, though, I doubt he appreciated my candor.

Our engineering casualties settled out after a few days underway and we returned to Norfolk two months later without further issues. After less than a week home, we headed to Yorktown to offload our weapons before entering the shipyard for what would be my final four months on board. On Friday afternoon, just prior to getting underway from the weapons station, I was summoned to the captain's cabin, where he told me that he had been notified we would be required to defuel the entire ship before entering the shipyard on Monday. This was a change from our earlier instructions, which had us defueling only the middle fuel bank. I immediately said that was no problem and set out to coordinate a barge so we could defuel the ship beginning first thing the next morning: Saturday.

I arrived early that Saturday morning and personally verified that our defueling valve alignment was proper. Given the maximum capacity of our defueling system and the amount of fuel that had to be off-loaded, I knew within the first hour that we would not be able to finish during daylight hours. I also knew that defueling after dark required the permission of the Senior Officer Present Afloat (SOPA) and the others involved in the transfer—the most important being my captain.

My first stop was to find the command duty officer. I informed him of the situation and asked that he give the captain a call to let him know while I continued to coordinate with the barge guys and tie up the other loose ends.

It was shortly after noon when one of my engineering duty petty officers came into the central control station from where I was monitoring the defueling to tell me our forward lube oil purifier had gone down. He was going to tear it apart in order to troubleshoot it. Since I was on board and the duty section was light on help for this petty officer, I said I wanted to assist him and proceeded to the forward engine room, where I remained until almost 10:00 p.m.

By the time I left the forward engine room and spent some time catching up with things in the central control station (CCS), the command duty officer had already gone to bed for the night.

We finally finished defueling the ship without issue at about 2:15 Sunday morning. I verified our defueling system was properly secured, made sure our underway check-off sheet was being followed for our Monday morning underway, and went home for the remainder of the weekend.

Early Monday morning we set our sea and anchor detail for our short transit to the shipyard in downtown Norfolk. As always, once all the engineering pre-underway checks were complete, I went to the pilothouse to report to the commanding officer that the engineering department was ready to get underway. As he took the check-off sheet from me and signed it, he asked, "Alan, when did you finish defueling the ship?" From those words, his tone, and the way his eyes were boring into me, I instantly knew that he had never been called about our defueling after sunset.

I said, "We finished at about two fifteen Sunday morning."

"Did it ever cross your mind to give me a call?"

"Yes, sir. It did," I replied.

The captain just shook his head, handed back my underway check-off sheet, and turned to go back inside the pilothouse.

As I walked back to the engineering spaces, I had the urge to track down the officer who had failed to call the captain and ask him what the hell he was thinking by not doing what he said he was going to, but ultimately, I was too mad at myself to blame anyone else. I knew I should have picked up the phone and called the captain myself on Saturday, and for the life of me I can't explain why I didn't.

I took my position in the central control station for the sea detail down the Elizabeth River, kicking myself for leaving that call up to the command duty officer. I should have known better, but by that point it was useless to even think about it.

Just prior to arriving at the shipyard, my electrical officer, who was serving as the helm safety officer on the bridge, called down to my engineering watch station and told me that he could hear another officer "sandbagging" me to the captain, telling the captain I'd taken his career into my hands by failing to call. My electrical officer said he believed I was going to be fired.

After almost two-and-a-half years on board, I would have expected some support from the other officer, rather than having him feed the captain's concerns. The officer knew me well and had to have known I would have never done anything intentionally to undermine or bypass the captain's authority. Rather than supporting me, though, he took control of the bus I had thrown myself under.

Sure enough, once we had tied up at our berth in the shipyard, I was summoned to the captain's cabin. On my way there, I stopped by the other officer's stateroom to ask if he knew what the issue was. I remember vividly how he sat at his desk, looking straight ahead and waving his right hand to shoo me off to the captain's cabin. He couldn't even look at me, knowing what I was about to walk into.

When I walked into the captain's cabin, he informed me that he was going to take disciplinary action against me but hadn't decided exactly what it would be. I knew the options ranged from a non-punitive letter of reprimand that wouldn't become a permanent part of my service record, to a punitive letter of reprimand or firing.

I returned to my stateroom at a complete loss. I sat down at my desk, thinking back to my hope of finishing my tour unscathed and with the captain's respect, and how that would never happen now. What had been the best two-and-a-half years of my career had all just been washed away because of one unintentional lapse in judgment that hadn't resulted in even the slightest mishap. While the benign outcome didn't excuse my failure to call the captain myself about the defueling running long, it did highlight the travesty of the situation.

I finished the day on the ship without calling home to give my wife a heads-up about what might happen. She had taken care of our daughter primarily by herself, and had left her life in New York to be with me, and I wasn't about to make her worry over the phone. When I walked through our door that night around 8:00 p.m., I sat down on the steps leading to the second floor, and for the first time since I had found that damn tepee, I put my face in my hands, feeling completely lost. Unlike when I was twelve, though, this time I didn't cry.

My wife approached me and asked what was going on. I told her I had probably made dozens of decisions, if not a hundred, every day without anyone above me giving me their input. I was responsible for so many decisions that involved the engineering plant, many of which if made incorrectly could kill someone or damage equipment. I took great care in each of those decisions, weighing and considering the input from my guys so as not to jeopardize the crew or the ship. Yet here I was, on the verge of being fired for something that never should have happened.

I guess it would have been an option (although not an easy one) to fight for myself by blaming the CDO who had said he was going to call the captain about defueling after dark, but that just wasn't who I was. I might have been about to lose my job, but I wasn't going to give up my self-respect to save it by blaming someone else for my own stupidity.

The next morning I stopped in to see the executive officer to tell him I was going to go talk to the captain about what happened. He told me to stay far away from the captain because he had expressed that he didn't want to lay eyes on me until he had decided what he was going to do. I exited the XO's stateroom, shut his door, and walked straight to the captain's cabin.

I knocked on the captain's door, went in, and said, "Captain, I just want you to know that what I did had nothing to do with a lack of respect for you or some misplaced loyalty to your predecessor. All I wanted for the six months we would be together was to earn your respect, and I feel that possibility is lost forever. I will take whatever punishment you decide is appropriate without comment or appeal."

He stood up from his desk, threw his ball cap on his credenza as he walked toward me, then hugged me and said, "Let's forget the whole thing." It was over that quickly. I was absolutely stunned. Perhaps his wife had said something the night before to soften his resolve, I don't know. But whatever the reason was, I wasn't going to complain.

A few days later all the department heads and the XO were in the captain's cabin for a morning meeting when the captain received a phone call from his wife. He barely said a word before hanging up the phone, turning to us, and saying, "Dad died. I'm leaving."

Although I had seen some things in my father I didn't agree with, at the time of his death, he was my best friend in many ways. I knew from my captain's reaction to the news of his father's death that they had been very close. That night after I got home and had dinner, I sat down and wrote the captain a letter—not a card, but a letter. Among other things, I expressed that I knew what it was like to lose a father and best friend in a single breath and how sincerely sorry I was for his loss.

When the captain returned from leave, I sensed an immediate change in how he interacted with me. He no longer left me his end-of-day discrepancy list. And, if he was in a meeting in his cabin when I knocked on the door, he ended the meeting immediately to talk with me. Our conversations and interactions seemed almost like father-to-son and vice versa.

Toward the middle of his first week back from emergency leave, his wife visited him on the ship. After her visit and after having said goodbye to the captain, she asked the officer of the deck to have me come to the quarterdeck. When I arrived she led me off to the side and said that I was the only one on the ship who had sent her husband anything regarding the death of his father, and how much my letter meant to him. She said he would never forget it. He never thanked me in words for the letter, but his actions said everything that mattered.

Those next few months as his engineer officer were the best of my tour. For the first time since college, I felt as if someone truly knew and liked the man I was. Thinking about that time with him, especially in light of that whole defueling experience, brings me great peace. It remains one of the most meaningful interpersonal experiences of my life.

∽

I finished that tour having learned some incredibly valuable lessons

I carried with me throughout the remainder of my career and still do today. Perhaps the most important of those lessons was that the pervasive opinion in the surface warfare officer community that the CO and XO should play the "good cop / bad cop" routine is complete garbage. That approach might have a place in a law enforcement interrogation room or at BUD/S, but it has no place in an organization that spends so much time espousing the benefits of positive leadership. While I served on *Thomas S. Gates*, I worked for three outstanding commanding officers and two equally impressive executive officers. This made *Gates* the best ship I had ever served on.

My department head tour also reaffirmed that I would always be who I was, no matter the circumstance or potential for severe consequences. Giving up self-respect to save yourself never leads to a satisfying outcome, and most times the punishment is far preferable to having to live with the knowledge that you compromised your integrity and values.

Lastly, that tour further reinforced that there was something special and unique about serving with people at sea. Although the conditions could be relentless and demanding, the environment helped forge an unbreakable bond—one I never fully appreciated until that time. I found that supporting those in my charge above all else was what mattered most to me. It certainly brought me unparalleled gratification. I realized the influence my people had on me and how each of them buoyed me, taking turns making me laugh and helping me to keep things in perspective. If I had ever been part of an organization whose collective positive outlook was self-sustaining, it was the engineering department on *Gates*.

CHAPTER THIRTEEN

THE NAVAL COMMAND AND STAFF COLLEGE

In November 1991 I completed my tour as engineer officer on *Gates* and reported to the Naval Command and Staff College in Newport, Rhode Island. I was there for a year to earn a master's degree in national security and strategic studies. Attended by all branches of the United States military as well as a few select students from other Allied nations' armed services, the war college experience was considered by the navy officers a welcome break from sea duty.

While the army and marine corps especially demanded academic excellence from those they sent to the war college, the navy seemed to tacitly recognize that their officers needed a break from sea duty more than they needed the added pressure of being honor graduates. At least that's how most of the navy students saw things. Regarding the rigors of the course, the mantra amongst most of the navy guys was, "It's only a lot of reading if you do it." So I arrived at the war college fully committed to following that mantra, and using that year as a time to make my family a higher priority than my grades. I didn't particularly like getting Cs, but I knew what level of effort I would have to expend in order to stay above that standard. In my way of thinking, "better" was the enemy of "good enough" for most things academic.

Shortly after starting my studies, my wife and I decided we wanted to expand our family, and a few months into the tour, we learned we would be having twins. Mike, my roommate from *Gates*, and I had remained in touch, and he found the news especially exciting, as he was a twin. Our calls would start with Mike calling me "Eschbaugh" and that whole routine. It never got old. And as they had so often on the *Gates*, our conversations ended with one of us recounting a sports story.

In May 1992, roughly sixth months into my time at the war college and only two days after our last conversation, I received notification from a close friend that Mike had died in an airplane mishap in Pensacola, Florida. Even now, more than twenty years later, I remember him vividly and have his picture on my desk as I type these words. I have never met anyone like him.

With the birth of our twins, Mary and Everett, in August 1992, my life got considerably busier. I was beginning the phase of my studies during which the weekly reading assignments sometimes totaled more than a thousand pages. Aside from work-related technical manuals or warfare publications, that was more pages than I usually read in a year. Even with the mantra *It's only a lot of reading if you do it*, I still had to complete the reading if I wanted to pass.

Once the twins began drinking formula, my wife and I would go to bed at 8:30 p.m. and then get up at midnight to feed them, each of us feeding one. After putting them back in their cribs, I would stay up for the remainder of the night and read until about 6:00 a.m. I would then shower and go to class for the day. Once I arrived home around 4:00 p.m., my sole focus was taking care of the kids. That became my daily routine Sunday through Thursday night and must have lasted for about a month until the twins began to sleep through the night.

Although I truly didn't care about getting more than an average grade, I still had to put in an effort that would allow me to accept whatever my grade turned out to be. I couldn't use my domestic responsibilities as an excuse to just squeak by. I felt out of control with the arrival of my twins, which was why I stayed up after midnight to read—unlike two growing infants, reading was something I could control. I actually ended up reading much more than I would have otherwise. As it turned out, that was the trimester in which I earned my highest grades.

By the time my year at the war college was over, I had been assigned the post of executive officer of USS *John S. McCain*, an *Arleigh Burke*-class guided missile destroyer being built in Bath, Maine.

CHAPTER FOURTEEN

USS *John S. McCain*

From my first day aboard *Pharris* until the day I stepped aboard USS *John S. McCain*, I don't remember once thinking about what it would be like to serve as the commanding officer. That possibility was just too far off into the future to feel even remotely possible. Even as I got closer to that possibility, I was too consumed with my responsibilities to think about anything beyond the next inspection or whatever else was at hand. So as I entered my tour as *McCain*'s second in command, my eyes and ears were finally wide-open to learning as much as I could in the event that I ever did get the chance to command at sea.

While I had served with many superb captains leading up to this tour, my captain on *McCain* was uniquely different from the rest. That man, Commander Jake Ross, and I had known each other for almost ten years and were good friends. It was Jake's influence with the placement officer that secured my assignment as his executive officer.

Jake was unique. He had an air of comfort in who he was that I found incredibly calming. Many people have confidence in their abilities—some are arrogant, some have no apparent reason for such self-confidence—but few of them seem truly comfortable. Jake was comfortable in every aspect of his life, and that included not being intimidated or insecure about his shortcomings. Ironically, looking at his career, you'd think that if anyone had reason for conceit or arrogance, it would be he. He had commanded a minesweeper through mine-seeded enemy waters at a very early stage in his career; he had been selected for promotion at least two years early; and he had recently completed a two-year tour as the naval aide to President George H. W. Bush. Yet Jake was completely devoid of arrogance. It was as if he didn't know who he was.

Jake told me right from the beginning that his job was to give me as much experience as he could so that when I became the commanding officer of a ship, no task or situation would be unfamiliar. Other captains I'd known might have wanted to treat their executive officers that way, but few of them had the courage to do it. Jake never said *if* I got to command. He always said *when*.

After *John S. McCain* was placed in service, I conned (drove) the ship for every special sea and anchor detail or evolution until Jake was convinced I could train and oversee the department heads and division officers. He would stay out of the pilot house until the absolute last second before we gave a "green deck" to land a helicopter, made our approach to an oiler, or singled up all lines prior to getting underway from the pier.

Jake also insisted that I be his principal assistant when it came to the ship's war fighting and operations. That meant my priorities were to become proficient as a mariner, and to understand how to employ the combat capabilities of *McCain*. On many ships the XO is in charge of administration, as well as the health and comfort of the crew. Jake's belief was that administration should be left up to the personnelmen and yeomen. My only administrative responsibility was to serve as the final reviewer before any paperwork was sent to him.

With regard to my development as a tactician and my increased understanding of the ship's impressive capabilities, Jake included me in all the decisions regarding his battle orders—orders that direct the employment of a ship's weapons and combat systems under various circumstances. For one of the most challenging missile firings during our fleet certification process, Jake allowed me to be the authority for weapons release while he watched from the pilothouse.

Jake also gave me considerable latitude in administering the ship's discipline—short of captain's mast. Aside from a few offenses he insisted on adjudicating, it was up to me to decide how to dispatch the crew's violations of the Uniform Code of Military Justice. I obviously briefed him on my decisions, but he supported every call I ever made. That trust gave me my first true sense of the authority the captain of a ship at sea holds. I found I would get sick to my stomach knowing my decision to forward a case to the captain could very possibly lead to a sailor's forfeiture of money, rank, or time spent with his family. I found that responsibility gut-wrenching and never took it lightly.

From a personal perspective, Jake was endlessly generous and gracious. When the ship was in port, I would get up at 3:00 a.m. and run six miles to the naval base in Honolulu—our homeport. I would go through the morning's message traffic, place it on his desk, and highlight the most important messages. Jake would arrive shortly after morning colors at 8:00. This allowed me time to get the daily plan under way. I'd go to his cabin upon his arrival, and he would insist I take a bottle of Gatorade from his refrigerator. Sometimes I think he stocked it primarily for my benefit. Later in the day, knowing I had three small children at home and how early I was getting up, Jake would come see me around 3:00 p.m. and tell me to go home. Maybe he did it in order to spend time on his ship without me getting in his way. I don't know, but I do know he couldn't have treated me any better than he did.

∽

Like every other tour I had before *McCain*, this one too presented a few opportunities for my past and my perspective to come through loud and clear. The first occurred while the ship was being built in Bath, Maine. My family and I lived in military housing just outside the naval air station in Brunswick. At the time of our arrival, our oldest child was twenty-seven months, and the twins were eight months. Needless to say, we had our hands full—especially my wife.

As the ship progressed through our manning and training phases, some of us spent more and more time away from Maine for training or to visit the pre-commissioning detachment in San Diego. During one of these trips out of town, my wife began receiving frightening phone calls from a man who was obviously watching—if not stalking—my family from an unknown vantage point. The man would say things like, "I saw you and Mary in the driveway today. She is really getting big."

Upon my return home, the calls would stop immediately. In fact, I had nearly forgotten about them by the time I left town again for another school—this one in Dahlgren, Virginia. My first night there I phoned home, and my wife told me the man had called again. I was now kicking myself for not knocking on every door in the neighborhood to see if anyone had ever noticed some whack job in the area.

In 1992 caller ID was not common. I certainly didn't have it. However, I knew such a device existed. I immediately called the ship's supply officer (SUPPO) and asked him to go by the house, pick up a check from my wife, go to Radio Shack, and purchase a caller ID box for our phone. SUPPO was more than happy to do it, and the new caller ID was hooked up within the hour.

The next day I phoned home and my wife informed me the man had called again. Although the caller ID didn't show his name, she had a number. I called the Brunswick Police Station to explain what was going on, and asked if they could run the phone number and take action against the man. They told me the only way they could do anything was if we could show on our phone records we had dialed *69 after receiving three calls from the man. Until such time they could do nothing.

Fortunately my training was ending soon, and I returned home. The first thing I did after walking through the door and hugging my family was grab the Brunswick area phone book and go through it entry by entry until I found the number. I waited until after dark and ran approximately four miles to the address corresponding with the phone number in the phone book. Once there, I hid just far enough away from the driveway not to be noticed, but close enough to see if anyone came to or left the house. I didn't see anyone, but the lights were on inside the house. I got closer and saw a man and woman inside. Both looked to be in their mid-sixties. I studied the man's face as best I could before running the four miles back home.

After a few days with no phone calls from him, I surmised he knew I was home. I began getting up earlier than normal and running to work. I left my car in the driveway unmoved from one day to the next. I wanted things to appear as they did when I was out of town. Sure enough, he called after just one day. My wife answered the phone, listened to his voice, and immediately turned the phone over to me. I remember every word I said to him: "Hello, Dick. I know who you are. I've been to your house, and I've called the police. If I see you or your pickup truck anywhere near my house, I will drive to your home and take every action necessary to make you sorry you ever decided to threaten my family."

I went on to describe the pictures on the wall of his den, his wife's appearance, and the chairs they sat in every night. By the time I finished, I was ready to drive to his house and forget waiting for the next time he called. He never said a word, but he also didn't hang up on me. That was the last time he ever phoned my house, and I hope it was the last time he ever harassed another family. Maybe I should have been named Maynard. I had certainly inherited my grandfather's protective gene.

∽

Another significant and unfortunate experience on *McCain* began to reshape my views on alcohol. The incident occurred during one of our trips to San Diego to visit our pre-commissioning detachment. While out to dinner on a Friday evening, Captain Ross and I were notified that one of our sailors had been shot outside of a nightclub. When we arrived at the hospital, our sailor was on life support. I remember standing behind the window to his room as his doctors evaluated his condition. At one point, I became very aware that I had had a beer or perhaps two during dinner, and I was now concerned that someone (either the doctor or the sailor's wife) would smell the alcohol on my breath. Even though I was not drunk, that awareness limited my ability to engage fully with everyone there. I felt as if I had let the sailor down because I couldn't fully support his family at that critical time.

Unfortunately our sailor did not recover from his wound. I remember sitting in my room at the bachelor officers' quarters later that night and thinking about how alcohol had influenced every aspect of that evening. Its consumption had facilitated the shooting, and it had impaired my ability to offer my full support to his family because it kept me at arm's length. That whole experience gave me great pause on the subject, and I began to evaluate the role, if any, I wanted alcohol to have in my life.

∽

On my final day aboard *John S. McCain*, Jake assembled the crew on the flight deck for my departure. Most times when an officer detaches, even the XO, it's only the officers who are assembled on the quarterdeck to say their goodbyes. But Jake had allowed me to give so much of myself to *his* crew, he knew how deep my bond had become with everyone. And again, because of how comfortable he was with himself, he didn't feel threatened in the least by someone else being liked and respected on his ship.

After presenting me with my end-of-tour award, which he wrote himself, and frocking me to commander, which was not in accordance with navy regulations, Jake handed me the microphone so I could say goodbye to everyone. This was another first for me: my first glimpse into how tough it would be leaving command.

By the time I detached from *John S. McCain*, I again felt like someone really knew who I was and appreciated it. But unlike the other times, I felt like my boss was also my friend. And unlike my other tours, it was the first tour during which I never had cause to take a stand against something I viewed as unreasonable. I learned more while on *John S. McCain* about the responsibilities of command than in all my other tours combined. More than anything though, I saw how the actions and example of one person can influence so completely an entire command.

CHAPTER FIFTEEN

The Pentagon

I reported to the navy staff at the Pentagon in June 1995 as the requirements officer for Standard Missile, the MK 41 Vertical Launching System, and the Advanced Combat Direction System.

I knew instantly this job was not a good fit for me, and for most of the next twenty-four months, I wished every single day of that existence away. Had I known how out of place and disinterested in the process of planning and budgeting I was going to be, I would have avoided that tour at all costs. As with many things, ignorance really was bliss in the months leading up to my arrival at the Pentagon.

My family and I found a house in Alexandria, Virginia, roughly eleven miles from the Pentagon. With the doors at north parking opening at 5:00 a.m., I quickly settled into the routine of arriving just as the doors opened and getting to my desk at 5:05 a.m. On most days, I left my office around 7:00 p.m. With my children all still under five years old, they would be asleep by the time I got home, so the only time I saw them awake was from Saturday morning until they went to bed on Sunday evening.

The mood in the Pentagon was morose and unfriendly—if not downright hostile. Only once in twenty-four months did I pass a stranger in the hallway who said hello first, responded to my greeting, or even smiled. The reason I recall the one exception is because as soon as we greeted each other and smiled, we both looked back over our shoulders in disbelief that someone had actually said hello.

∽

The relentless, never-ending paperwork battles inside the Pentagon left most of us in the surface warfare directorate without even a shred of the gratification we were so used to enjoying at sea. We had no sailors or division officers to take care of, and we had few things (if any) that were completely up to us to decide. I had come from being second-in-command of a guided missile destroyer where I had weapons release authority on the most challenging missile exercise in our navy, but in my position at the Pentagon, I couldn't decide on the font size or the color of a PowerPoint slide. To say it was frustrating is a colossal understatement.

After wishing about a year of my life away, I went to my boss and said something had to give. I wasn't seeing my family, I hated my job, and I could see virtually no value in the work I was spending so much time doing. I was finally unwilling to continue doing that. Life is too short to live the way I had been living. Fear of not screening for command at sea didn't concern me one iota.

I was used to long hours. It wasn't the time in the office that made me miserable; it was what I considered to be the unreasonable expectations and demands of my boss. In my position as an action officer, nothing was left up to me. Everything had to be done his way, with no allowance for original thought. Although I genuinely liked the man and knew him to be a gentleman socially, it was just his personality to leave nothing to chance. Had his approach proved valid during that first year, I would have never considered questioning his method, but after a year of producing mountains of paperwork that never left his office, I was done wasting my time doing things that I knew were serving no purpose or greater good.

I had long understood that any time I had an issue accepting the leadership style of my boss, the issue could be primarily mine—not theirs. Therefore, every time I approached confrontation I did it from the position of going in and trying to figure out why the person was making the demands they made. I truly wanted to hear their perspectives, knowing it would help me better understand and come to accept their leadership styles. So when I found myself in the situation I was in at the Pentagon, I went to my boss's office and said, "I hate my job and I'm not seeing my family. I refuse to hate my life so much that I'm wishing every second of it away. If you can't help me find a way to support you in a manner that gets the job done *and* gives me some job satisfaction, I'm going to start coming in every day at eight, and I'm leaving at five."

I went on to ask for some latitude and autonomy in how we answered our tasking, because I felt as if that would at least give me some satisfaction, but he politely said he couldn't do it—not that he *wouldn't*, but that he *couldn't*. Just as I knew who I was, he also knew who he was. He did attempt a small concession by telling me he would try not to micromanage me as much.

Although I knew it was the best he could offer, I said it wasn't good enough. I knew if I left it at that, I would be right back in there within two days. He was unable and unwilling to move beyond that concession, so for the next two days, I came in at 8:00 a.m., ran at lunchtime, and then left at 5:00 p.m.—just as I had promised. As I passed his office on the morning of the third day, he called me into his office and said, "I spoke to my wife about your comments and she agrees with you. So from now on I'd like to ask that you start coming in at your previous time. In the afternoon, if you are here after eighteen hundred (6:00 p.m.) that's on you. On Fridays if you are here after fifteen hundred (3:00 p.m.), that's on you. I'm going to have this same conversation with everyone in the office."

Things changed immediately. Even though my hours went back to what they had been prior to our confrontation, the mood in the office dramatically improved. True to his word, each evening at 6:00, he would yell out and remind us all we were now in the office because we felt we needed to be there, and each Friday afternoon, he would do the same at 3:00. Although that man outranked me and would have been well within his authority to end my upward mobility, he cared enough about *how* the job was getting done to accept the possibility that his method needed some adjustment. His willingness to make that effort made me want to work for him with a passion I had never had before. I know that confronting the wrong person could have led to my firing, but trying to find some enjoyment in the fourteen hours a day I spent at work was more important than keeping my job.

∽

I know that some people, especially many in the military, feel it's never appropriate or justified to question superiors. And while I know there are times and circumstances that don't allow it, I do believe there are times when those questions can and should be asked. I approached my boss in the most professional way I knew how, and I would like to believe it positively impacted those who served with him after that. For me, I needed to have a better reason than just the fact that he was my boss to work for him. His willingness to look at himself and adjust his tactics provided that reason.

I always welcomed questions regarding my methods from anyone who wanted to hear my rationale, because sometimes when I heard myself explain my decision out loud, I realized it didn't sound like such a wise decision after all. When that happened, I had no problem acknowledging it, and also identifying and crediting the person whose question led to my enlightenment. If leaders want to be the best they can be, and if they have faith in their methods, they should be open to questions about those methods. And if leaders truly care about their people, why wouldn't they be open to exploring and acknowledging the aspects of their personalities that are counterproductive? There have been many times when I forgot to reflect on my negative tendencies, but fortunately I had convinced people to be honest with me if they felt I was being unreasonable.

Leaders who can't handle considering the notion that they might be the problem are most likely being compelled by fear or insecurity. If they had more confidence in their approaches, they would be less defensive when confronted about them. More often than not, negative leaders are unaware of, or don't care enough to consider, the impact their demands or actions are having on their officers and crews. If those leaders are never approached, that will never change, and people will continue to wish days—if not years—of their lives away. I value my time far too much to live that way.

CHAPTER SIXTEEN

NAVAL SURFACE FORCE, ATLANTIC

I detached from my tour at the Pentagon almost exactly two years from the day I reported. Although I had screened for command at sea during that tour, I still had one more stop before I began the training pipeline leading to command.

The next year flew by. Unlike my time in the Pentagon, I now loved both my job and my boss. That job, Flag Secretary for the Commander, Naval Surface Force, Atlantic, was a lot like being the XO again. I was close enough to the top to see what the boss and his chief of staff thought about important issues that impacted ships and sailors, but I really wasn't responsible for anything aside from reviewing point papers and other similar administrative duties. It was also a great job because the admiral for whom I worked had been one of my commanding officers on *Thomas S. Gates*. As well as he knew me, I was somewhat shocked when he selected me for his staff.

Within a few months of reporting, I was officially slated to assume command of USS *Arleigh Burke* (DDG 51). Even though my boss was reluctant to insert himself into the process of assigning officers to ships, I believe my opportunity to command a ship had much to do with him. Not because he made any calls on my behalf, but because he was so highly respected by those responsible for assigning officers to specific ships, that I don't doubt they tried to take care of those working for him.

Had I been given the choice of any ship to command, *Arleigh Burke* would have been my choice, without question. Although it was the oldest ship in the class of roughly twenty-five at the time, in my mind it was the most special. The ship and the class were named after Admiral Arleigh A. Burke, at the time the only person to ever serve three terms as the Chief of Naval Operations. Admiral Burke had done so much for the navy during his career, and because of his and his wife's generosity, he continued to give to the ship and her sailors even after their deaths.

∽

The Prospective Commanding Officer (PCO) pipeline can cover a somewhat extended period of time if your schedule allows. For those officers going to an Aegis-class destroyer or cruiser, the pipeline includes a six-week stop in Dahlgren, Virginia, in addition to the other schools all prospective commanding officers attend. It was during my stop in Dahlgren that I was faced with a decision that could have been career ending, depending on how it was interpreted by my detailer.

When I left Virginia Beach to begin my class in Dahlgren, my wife was about to start the final phase of her teaching certification. She had already completed all of the academic work and had passed her Praxis exams, needing only six weeks of student teaching experience to finish the certification requirements.

Her first day of class happened to coincide with my first day in Dahlgren. At the end of the day, I called home, and for the first time since I'd known her, my wife seemed a bit frazzled. Even when the man in Maine was stalking her, or the many times she was left alone to care for three children, she never seemed overwhelmed or unsure of how to proceed. So, hearing the stress in her voice that night, I knew something was wrong.

On that first day of student teaching, one of the twins, almost six at the time, had woken up very sick and unable to go to school. My wife phoned a number of friends before finally finding one able to watch our daughter for the day. My wife arrived almost four hours late for her first day on the job—not the way she'd wanted to start.

The next day was even worse, and this time, my wife was unable to find anyone to watch our daughter. Fortunately, I had called home first thing that day to see how things were going and checked in again during my first break, when I found my wife completely at her wit's end. Without making any promises, I hung up the phone and walked straight to the commanding officer's office of the school I was attending. I introduced myself to his secretary and asked if I could have a moment with the captain.

I had only ever seen the captain during his welcome remarks to our class the day before, and I had no idea how he would react to what I was about to say, but I honestly wasn't concerned. I was going to do exactly what I needed to do, regardless of whether I had his permission. It wasn't that I didn't respect him or his position. It was because the worst-case scenario would be losing my opportunity to command a ship, and I knew there were worse things in life. As important as my naval career was to me, supporting someone who had supported me for the last nine years was more important.

After introducing myself, I simply said, "My family needs me. I'm going home."

I told him I would contact the detailer and tell him of my plans, and if allowed I would try to find another time to come back to the school. The captain didn't ask any questions. He simply said, "Okay." With that, I checked out on leave and drove home.

My detailer was equally supportive, and so for the next six weeks, I cared for my three children for the first extended period of time in their young lives. Those six weeks with my children were the most rewarding and enjoyable of any time I spent with them before or after. It was amazing. My wife finished her student teaching in time for me to pick up my next class, and the rest of my pipeline went without issue.

Part IV

USS *Arleigh Burke*

"Our lives begin to end the day we become silent about things that matter."

— Dr. Martin Luther King Jr.

CHAPTER SEVENTEEN

Turning Over with a Good Friend

On the morning of October 11, 1999, I reported aboard USS *Arleigh Burke* to begin my turnover with my good friend and former shipmate, Nevin Carr. With the exception of my father, grandfather, and Captain Ross, everyone who had influenced my life growing up was present four days later for the change of command—including Davie, Eddie, Ed Wenger, and Coach Harrington. Even most of my cousins and friends were in attendance.

Command at sea is quite unique in both the level of autonomy and the breadth of responsibility. If a person were to ever sit down and think about its enormity, they might actually have reason for pause before accepting the role. Although I knew there would be plenty of things I would learn on the job, I wasn't nervous about discovering them. More than anyone, I had Captain Ross to thank for that.

One of the things arranged for me to accomplish during the week of our turnover was an office call with our destroyer squadron commodore. When I was led into the commodore's office, he stood and invited me to sit down at his conference table. The next two minutes were unlike any interview I had ever had. Although I don't remember every word, the interview went something like the following.

It began with both of us sitting down and just staring at each other. After a few seconds, he took a deep breath, exhaled, and offered me two sentences of his philosophy. It was so loosely put together, I don't think I'd even call it a philosophy. It was something along the lines of, "Stay in school, and don't do drugs." That wasn't what he said, but it might as well have been. Then he took another deep breath, exhaled, and fell silent.

Feeling it was my turn to say something, I said, "I'll do my best not to screw it up." Laying out a lot of bullshit about all the great things I was going to do just wasn't my style. It would be like telling my new baseball coach I was going to hit .400 for the year. Don't tell someone what you're going to do, just do it. They'll find out soon enough how good or bad you are.

After my quick sound burst, we both simultaneously inhaled and exhaled in unison, and then just stared at each other. I finally broke that stretch of silence with, "Okay, sir, it was nice to meet you." And with that I got up, we shook hands, and I left. As I walked out of the building I smiled to myself and thought, *We're going to get along just fine.*

I couldn't have been more correct in my initial assessment of the commodore. He turned out to be an awesome boss. He let me run the ship—in fact, he expected me to run the ship. As we got to know each other, I learned that he had seen combat, so his perspective on those things in life that truly mattered was obviously tempered by his past experiences. Although we talked less frequently than you might expect someone to speak with one's boss, he couldn't have been more supportive.

∽

The five days or so I spent turning over, and more importantly spending time with Nevin before he left, were some of the most enjoyable days of my career. I did my best to get off the ship early most days, and to hang around no more than absolutely necessary in order to allow Nevin some final time alone with his officers and crew. I knew in this case that I was "the other man" about to steal *his* wife and children.

Our change of command was held on Marion's forty-third birthday, October 15, 1999. My former boss from my days at Surface Force, Atlantic, was kind enough to serve as our principal speaker. This made the event even more special because both Nevin and I had been two of the admiral's department heads on *Thomas S. Gates*. With quite a few of the other department heads and division officers in attendance, it felt like a *Gates* reunion.

As is customary for the incoming commanding officer, I kept my remarks brief. In fact, they couldn't have been more than about sixty seconds—if that long. I thanked everyone for coming, thanked Nevin for such a professional turnover, and then told the officers and crew that I wished they could feel what I felt in my heart, because if they could, they would know how proud and honored I was to be their captain. With that, I took over as USS *Arleigh Burke*'s sixth commanding officer.

CHAPTER EIGHTEEN

MY FIRST CHALLENGE

In an effort to get to know the leadership on *Arleigh Burke* as quickly as possible, I decided to have lunch every day with one of my officers or chief petty officers until I had met with each individually. Given the number, it would take me a few months to eat with all of them. As the end of every lunch approached, I asked what he or she thought I could do to make the ship even better. With only one exception, all the chief petty officers told me there was a sailor who had recently reported aboard who was already becoming a menace, and asked that I do something about it. The situation was so uniquely appalling, no one had the courage to attempt to handle it themselves. I recall seeing this sailor checking in on the same day that I reported to the ship, so there was no way Nevin could have known he'd be a problem.

Without going into all the details, I'll say that this sailor's behavior was aggressive and threatening and effectively made life very uncomfortable for anyone who dared to confront him regarding his actions. It was impossible not to notice his disposition. It wasn't so much that he was defiant. It was more that he could not have cared less about what anyone else said or thought, and seemed happy to make everyone miserable by terrifying them. Although I had my suspicions, I never knew if he had some sadistic motive behind his actions, only that he was incessantly hostile and antagonistic with all but a few people on board.

He was physically intimidating as well. Having seen some very fit SEALS when I was at BUD/S, I was hard to impress when it came to physical fitness, but this man did some things I had never seen anyone do before. On a few occasions in the ship's workout area, I would see him exercising. For the entire thirty minutes I was using a cardio machine, he did sit-ups at a pace that most people could maintain for a two-minute physical fitness test at best. He easily did 1,300 sit-ups straight, showing virtually zero effort or strain aside from a steady stream of sweat pouring off his forehead.

Although he was in exceptional shape, I noticed right away he had some physical conditions that should have disqualified him from sea duty. I called my corpsman and had him bring me the sailor's medical record so I could find out exactly what his medical issues were. It didn't take long to see there was no possible way this man was fit for sea duty, yet his record included a fitness for sea duty report that had been approved by a navy doctor less than a year earlier.

I phoned the doctor who had signed the report and asked him about it. Without hesitation, the doctor responded, "I remember him perfectly, and he's not fit for sea duty."

I was flabbergasted, and I asked the obvious question, "Then why did you say he was?"

The doctor told me the sailor's former commanding officer had called him on the sailor's behalf and told him he was a "water walker" (like Jesus, though if that were true, the resemblance ended there) and deserved to be found fit for sea duty.

Now things were beginning to make sense. The sailor had put in a request to split his sea tour between multiple ships, so per navy policy, the only way he could leave his first ship was to be evaluated as fit for continued sea duty. His commanding officer had obviously been having the same issues with him I was having now on *Arleigh Burke*. All that captain had wanted was to see the sailor leave, so he said and did whatever was necessary to make that happen without feeling threatened.

I couldn't do that. As far as I was concerned, the good order and discipline of the ship was my responsibility, and this sailor's actions undercut those priorities. I probably should have been at least a little wary of this man, but just as defending my brother was easy when I was young, so too was taking a stand for the ship.

I had the sailor come to my cabin and told him I considered his actions on the ship incongruent with good order and discipline. I said I was ordering him to undergo a fitness for sea duty evaluation where there would be no stacking of the deck. I informed him that most likely, he would be found unfit and rotated ashore until he could retire.

I knew trying to document his behavior in an effort to build a case for his administrative separation would be difficult and certainly a long, painful road. Therefore, I elected against that course of action. I knew it would have consumed too much time and prevented the ship from being what I needed it to be now.

The sailor was indeed found unfit for sea duty, and he transferred ashore without issue, or so I thought. A short while later, *Arleigh Burke* went to sea. Upon my return home, my wife told me about the almost nightly phone calls she'd received from someone spewing ugly, creepy thoughts. I knew instantly who was making those calls. In a way it was Brunswick, Maine, all over again. I told my XO to phone the command where my former sailor was stationed and get word to him that I wanted to see him in my cabin as soon as possible.

When the sailor walked in, I shut the door behind him so it was just the two of us. He stood there with a smirk on his face as if to say, "Now what are you going to do?" I spoke nearly the same words I had spoken to Dick about six years earlier, and I could tell right away he knew I was serious. The calls stopped immediately.

CHAPTER NINETEEN

FORMING NEW BONDS

Even when you're the captain, being the new guy on a ship presents some interesting dynamics with the recently inherited officers and crew. Whether intentionally or subconsciously, ship personnel have a hard time accepting a new captain. It's especially tough when the relieved captain was as revered as my predecessor.

No two commanding officers are alike. Everyone has different standards, priorities, preferences, pet peeves, and idiosyncrasies. The bond formed between the captain and crew is typically very strong because they serve together in arduous conditions. Even if most of the crew and officers are happy with a change of leadership, it still almost always requires modifying their routines somewhat in order to conform to the new captain's expectations and demands.

For a ship's new captain, things really start to change for the better when those officers and chiefs who have been on the ship the longest detach and are replaced by "your" guys. It's not that the old guard doesn't support the new captain. It's just that it can be exhausting, especially for department heads, to adjust to a new commanding officer. And until the commanding officer gets their new line of leaders, the team never truly feels like their own. On *Arleigh Burke*, things really started to come together after the last of my department heads changed out.

One of our final hurdles before beginning the advanced phase of our underway training was a comprehensive equipment inspection. The one we were about to have tested every piece of equipment and machinery used aboard the ship. An inspection team consists of a senior 0-6 (captain) and dozens of other very experienced and seasoned engineers of all specialties. They descend on the ship and conduct every possible test on the equipment to ensure and then document that everything is performing within designed parameters and standards. Nothing is excluded.

Aside from getting to know my officers and crew, the first priority I had on the ship was to push the time of that inspection out a few months to the nine-month point in my tour. That way I would have the time I needed to inspect every zone on the ship at least twice before the inspection was held. I knew the ship was in good shape when I took over, but having been an engineer as a department head and having been through three of these inspections prior to *Arleigh Burke*, I had some very specific expectations and a vision for where I wanted us to be for the inspection.

By the time we had the inspection, I was comfortable with our preparation and had every confidence we would do just fine. Aside from one major issue, which was quickly remedied by my guys, the inspection went well.

I had been pretty tough and demanding during my zone inspections in the nine months leading up to the inspection, and I knew some of my people thought I might have been unreasonable in my standards. However, with the good inspection results, the crew seemed to finally see my demands were reasonable. They also learned that the only standards that truly mattered were our standards—and this inspection validated that position. It made the crew really start to feel as if the ship was now ours. It was a definite turning point for us as a team.

CHAPTER TWENTY

Pre-Deployment Workups

Life as the captain of a ship at sea was unlike anything I had ever known. Even as the executive officer of *John S. McCain,* I had never truly understood the wide range of emotions that came with the territory of command. Although I knew the job had the potential to make one feel isolated and alone, I really never found it to be that way. If those moments ever began to settle in, I'd simply grab my ball cap and head up to the bridge or somewhere else where I could interact with the crew.

I also found that once we started to spend more time at sea in preparation for our upcoming deployment, I began to feel closer to the crew and wardroom. I had long held the opinion that unless two people have served at sea together, they really don't know each other. A person can hide a lot while in port because the end of the day allows them to go home, rest, and come back with a clear mind. At sea, though, there is no escape from that environment's demands—not the grind, not the fatigue, and certainly not the close living quarters with hundreds of other people. Throughout my career, if asked whether I knew someone, I always qualified my response with whether or not I had served with that person at sea. Being at sea with my ship and crew opened the floodgates to greater camaraderie.

Going to sea also gave me a chance to follow through on some of the promises I had made to the crew when I first arrived. The biggest of those was that if they had personal things they wanted to be present for ashore and the events occurred during one of our pre-deployment underway periods, I would allow them to stay ashore, provided we had people qualified to execute their duties. This is not standard practice on ships. The policy is normally that if the ship is underway, everyone is on it unless somewhere ashore on official orders. To me that policy was an example of making things black or white, which took the fun and gratification out of leadership. Why not explore new ways to make a positive impact?

In my mind, there was more to be gained by allowing someone to stay behind to support their family than by making them get underway, especially when the ship could do without that person for a short time. Sailors already sacrifice a great deal to serve their country. Why not recognize them for it with something substantial? There were some requests I didn't approve or allow, but I was always happy to explain my rationale. If it turned out I was wrong, I changed my mind. If people know that even when they reason with you, you'll never consider another point of view, they'll stop approaching you. Getting underway for deployment was not open for discussion except in special circumstances, so my atypical gesture of allowing people to miss underway periods when appropriate did a great deal to earn the crew's loyalty. More importantly, though, I felt it was the right thing to do. When that's your guiding principle, good outcomes tend to follow.

When it came to the work I oversaw, there were many things I considered a complete waste of time, and on which I didn't expend one bit of energy; however, I expected those things I felt were important to be done flawlessly. Being clear about which things were important to me made life fairly easy for the officers and crew. That didn't mean I wasn't demanding; I was. But I didn't make my people do things that weren't important to our readiness. My crew knew early on that everything on the ship that dealt with safety, navigation, weapons firings, watch standing, security, and safeguarding classified materials all had to be done in perfect compliance with the respective guidelines and standards. However, misspelling a word on a message and not catching the mistake until after it was transmitted didn't upset me unless it became a common occurrence, which it never did.

∽

Once our basic phase of training and our major inspections were out of the way, we were finally cleared to do what all sailors enjoy most—go to sea and continue training. How we trained would be left up to us to decide, and our standards would be the ones we tried to attain and then maintain, which was exactly how I wanted it. We had endured a good nine months of having to meet someone else's standards, and now it was our turn to take what we had learned and use it.

As had been the case for me in some earlier commands, things couldn't have lined up much better than they did on *Arleigh Burke*. I inherited a great ship with a professional crew, and I was part of a six-ship destroyer squadron with some truly good officers and friends in command of those ships. Just as the transfer of some of my longer-tenured officers and crewmembers opened the doors for new, energetic replacements, so too did the transfer of some of the longer-tenured commanding officers in our destroyer squadron. It allowed the new commanding officers to bond as we worked up together for deployment.

About the same time the last of the squadron commanding officers changed out, so did our strike group commander and his chief of staff. The new chief of staff had been the commanding officer of the guided missile cruiser in our strike group, so his transfer came without the angst that typically occurs when that position changes out. He knew all the destroyer and frigate commanding officers, and he was essentially a mentor to all of us.

The cruiser commanding officer in a strike group holds a unique role if he or she has the personality to embrace it. It's not unusual for a commanding officer to hesitate or shy away from fully exposing his weaknesses to the commodore—the boss. If the commanding officer of the cruiser is approachable and puts himself out there as an advocate for the destroyer and frigate captains, he can offer invaluable advice without having to worry about looking stupid to his boss. Our cruiser commanding officer was just that kind of man. When he was relieved from his duties as captain of the cruiser and went to the staff, his replacement was exactly that type of man as well.

The last leadership piece of the strike group that would take us on deployment and through our final pre-deployment certifications was the commander of our strike group. We couldn't have been more fortunate with ours.

When you are a commanding officer of a destroyer or frigate, the strike group commander might as well be the President of the United States, because while you are still trying to find your way as the captain of your first ship, they first served in command a full decade earlier and have forgotten more about command than you know. In their presence, no matter how gracious they are, their position as commander of a carrier strike group can be very intimidating.

Our new strike group commander was quite possibly the nicest flag officer I had ever met. After our initial introduction, he always asked about my family at subsequent meetings. He remembered and used the names of my wife and children and even knew their ages. He encouraged all of his commanding officers to spend time with our families before we deployed. In fact, he expected it. I remember coming across the quarterdeck one morning at about 8:15, and being told by my XO that the admiral had phoned and needed me to call him. When I got on the phone with the admiral, he asked me where I had been, and when I said I had walked my children to school, he replied, "Good for you." And he meant it.

During our underway periods, he would email me, as I am certain he did all of his commanding officers, to compliment the ship for our performance. Later, while on deployment, when we would be in different geographic locations, he would email me just because we hadn't talked in a week or so and he wanted me to know he hadn't forgotten us.

As our strike group began our final underway training exercise, all the leadership pieces were in place for deployment. For all the things *Arleigh Burke* did—including being the first ship in years to be cleared to shoot naval gunfire support at the Island of Vieques, firing every variant of missile on board, and executing the most challenging seamanship evolutions—I never once felt pressure from my chain of command. That confidence from the top and the freedom to do things as I thought best were more rewarding than I could have ever imagined. They allowed me to apply all the lessons I had learned from my past without concern that I was being watched or scrutinized at every turn.

∞

For years I loved being on the ship's bridge, so mentoring the junior officers on the skills associated with being a professional mariner brought me great enjoyment. I know some commanding officers stay off the bridge as much as possible to allow their junior officers freedom to act without feeling constantly watched by their captains, but I told my people right from the start that my presence on the bridge was because I loved being there—not because I didn't trust them. My being on the bridge so often gave the officers and sailors standing watch an opportunity to get comfortable in my presence. Consequently, when it was time to call me to make a required report, they did so without hesitation. Some even confessed they looked forward to it.

I once had a young officer named Tim Fox call me to the bridge after taps (10:00 p.m.). He got me on the phone and said, "Hey, Captain. Can you come to the bridge for a minute?"

I said, "Sure. Are you okay?"

"Yes, sir. I just want to show you something."

I had been sitting in my cabin working on a crossword puzzle in my sweats, so I threw on my boots and ball cap and went up to the bridge. When I got there, I asked the bridge watch team where Mr. Fox was, and they said he was on the bridge wing. When I walked out, I said, "What's up, Tim?"

Tim said to me, "Look at the stars, Captain. Aren't they incredible?"

He went on to tell me that when he was a boy, he would climb out of his bedroom window, look up at the stars, and imagine himself on a ship's bridge wing doing what we were doing now at sea.

I loved that one of my officers wanted to share those thoughts with me and that he wasn't hesitant to call me after taps just to see and enjoy a view that was special to him.

∽

By now being in command of *Arleigh Burke* was far and away the best job I had ever had. Although I had bosses, I wasn't micromanaged in the least. It was mind-boggling to think that only a few years earlier, I hadn't had the authority to decide how to write a point paper or a one-line, useless message. Now I was entrusted to take a one-billion-dollar warship wherever the country ordered me to go and to fight the ship as I saw fit within the rules of engagement and the law of armed conflict. Even thinking about it now makes me shake my head.

Every day of command at sea brought with it a new sense of camaraderie and commitment to the crew, the officers, and Admiral Burke's memory. The crew all seemed to take immense pride in the ship, and it showed in everything we did. My officers had confidence in their abilities, and often when I heard them interact with one of their chiefs or sailors, it reminded me of myself. It was so gratifying and would only get better.

One of the most important aspects of command that I learned from my second commanding officer on *Thomas S. Gates* was the value of the ship's zone inspection program. The surface force commander mandated that at least once every quarter, the commanding officer inspect every space and program on the ship. It doesn't sound like an overly demanding requirement, but to do it right takes a considerable amount of time and attention.

Some commanding officers execute this requirement by assembling all the chiefs and officers in the wardroom once a quarter and assigning them different spaces on the ship to inspect that day. Others, such as my second captain on *Gates*, did it all himself. Although both approaches get the entire ship inspected, the standards of the chiefs and officers doing the inspection vary widely. In my experience and opinion, the first approach only serves to check off a box and does very little to impact the material condition and readiness of the ship.

I did as was done on *Gates* and had the ship divided into twelve zones. Each week for twelve consecutive weeks, I inspected one zone. I expected the division officer and chief of that space to come along with me, while the space petty officer presented each space. Doing the inspection this way gave me a chance to interact with virtually everyone on the ship. Although I was considered pretty brutal for the first three months, the ship quickly learned what my standard was, and, by the second time through, the guys were proud to show off what they had been doing to improve since my last inspection. It was amazing the immediate, positive impact that extra attention had on the daily material readiness of the ship. By doing the inspections so religiously, we avoided those dips in readiness that often occur when spaces aren't regularly inspected. These inspections also built even more camaraderie on the ship, and crewmembers would frequently stop me in passing and ask me to come see their latest projects.

Our final pre-deployment exercise was known as Joint Task Force Exercise (JTFEX). This was a comprehensive battle problem primarily designed to certify our strike group commander and his staff for deployment. Our roles as ships in the strike group were simply to execute the many plans and courses of action decided upon by the admiral and his staff. My ability as a ship's captain, although always on display and at risk, had already been assessed by this point.

Toward the middle of this exercise, we received word that USS *Cole* had been attacked while in port in Aden, Yemen. In my time in the navy, this was a watershed event in so many ways. Most significant was that it brought the reach of international terrorism inside our lifelines.

Immediately after receiving the news, I contacted my strike group chief of staff and told him that if a ship from our battle group needed to leave early for deployment to replace *Cole*, *Arleigh Burke* was ready, and we wanted to go. Next I addressed the crew and informed them of the attack on *Cole* and that I had volunteered *Arleigh Burke* to head east immediately. I had such confidence in my relationship with the crew that I knew they would all be in agreement with that. I also asked them to keep all communication with their families devoid of anything regarding our schedule and to advise their families not to jump to conclusions. Once things settled down, I wrote my wife an email that I printed out and saved in my journal.

I remember vividly the day we got back to Norfolk after that exercise. The family turnout was especially large—most likely because of the attack on *Cole* and the uncertainty facing our deployment. In light of the developments in the Middle East the previous month, there was an abnormally high level of anxiety among the local media and the families getting ready to send their loved ones off to that region. As I had done for some time in command, I stood on the bridge wing high above the pier and watched the families come down and meet their sailors. I absolutely loved seeing those happy reunions with kids running to their parents and the spouses patiently standing back and waiting their turns. Of the many aspects of being in command at sea, I miss that opportunity perhaps the most. It felt so good knowing I had at least some small part in making that reunion possible.

CHAPTER TWENTY-ONE

DEPLOYMENT

With almost fourteen months in command behind me, we finally deployed the week after Thanksgiving of 2000. The presidential election was still in question, as the whole "hanging chad" situation had yet to play out. As was always my practice, I spent the night before deployment on the ship. I hate good-byes, and from the time I was a department head, I felt more comfortable on the ship the night before we got underway than I did being at home.

The weeks before a deployment are stressful—especially for families and people in relationships. Many people subconsciously pushed those closest to them away rather than keeping them close and allowing them to see or sense their anxiety over the looming separation. For me, I had to say my good-byes early and then get to the ship, where I could focus solely on making sure we were ready to go in the morning. Had I stayed home that last night, my thoughts would have been on the ship anyway. Going to the ship early saved my family from having to deal with me being on edge.

I set my alarm for 0400 the next morning to give myself time to interact with the duty section and to watch and greet my sailors as they reported to the ship. As I walked along the pier where *Arleigh Burke* was berthed, I remember looking at the ship and my sailors getting ready and thinking to myself that I was the luckiest person alive to be their captain. The privilege of deploying with them more than offset how much I was going to miss my family.

∞

The seas for our transit across the Atlantic Ocean were very rough. The aircraft carrier and the cruiser took one track across the Atlantic, while the smaller destroyers and frigates took another track that was a little less intense, but rough just the same. With quartering seas, our every-other-day refuelings were a little more challenging than usual, but I had the best master helmsmen I had ever seen, and they made those difficult conditions seem routine.

Our group of destroyers and frigates passed through the Strait of Gibraltar just as dawn was giving way to sunrise. Each of the four ships in our group had different places to head to from there. It was sad parting ways with the people I had spent so much time with underway and working up to deployment. Once again, my situation couldn't have been better with respect to the other commanding officers in my destroyer squadron. Each was professional and always willing to help a fellow commanding officer.

It was no secret to any of them that I was especially good friends with Commander Stephen Hampton, the commanding officer of USS *Deyo*. Steve and I had been department heads together on *Thomas S. Gates,* where Steve relieved Nevin as the operations officer. For anyone who knew him, Steve was a uniquely talented and passionate officer. He was relentless in his commitment to training his crew to fight and ensuring *Deyo*'s weapons systems were finely tuned and always operating at their designed performance levels.

For all our underway periods together, Steve and I always found a way to communicate and commiserate privately via a radio circuit. Those chats were priceless. We would discuss any uncertainty we might be having about how to execute a certain task or evolution and then come up with the right plan of attack in advance. We exchanged thoughts about underway replenishment courses given the rough seas and a number of other relevant topics. More often than not, the talks served simply to validate what we already knew were the best courses of action, and so those conversations were mostly just an excuse for us to talk to one another.

On that morning when we cleared the Strait of Gibraltar, I knew it would be the last time Steve and I would be geographically co-located while in command. *Arleigh Burke* was headed off to the Arabian Gulf, and Steve was staying in the Mediterranean Sea with *Deyo*. Serving in command within the same destroyer squadron with such a good friend made that experience even more special. I called Steve on the radio, had him kick to our usual, unused frequency, and thanked him for everything he had done for me during those last fourteen months. I wished him a safe deployment and said goodbye. Steve had become my confidant and sounding board for my most important command issues. It was like leaving my family all over again.

Although we stopped in Gibraltar and then Toulon, France, for port visits, our ultimate mission was to support operations in the Arabian Gulf. We sailed from Toulon just after Christmas, a day early, to avoid the worst of the mistral winds, which were forecasted to impede our transit. As we headed east toward the Suez Canal, the winds were on our quarter and seemed to follow us across the Mediterranean Sea. Transiting with us was an oiler dedicated to replenishing us until we anchored at Port Said. Each morning the master of the oiler and I would get on the radio and discuss the risk of refueling that day, ultimately deciding to refuel every day because we couldn't be certain that the seas would be any better the next day, and they might be even worse.

By the time we arrived at the anchorage area just outside of Port Said, it was late afternoon on the day before our transit south through the canal. We could tell things were still quite tenuous since the attack on *Cole*. With our readiness ever keen, we kept watchful eyes on every ship that came to anchor and every small craft transiting to and from the port.

⁓

I was very fortunate on *Arleigh Burke* to serve with two outstanding executive officers. The first, Commander Ed Mullen, transferred roughly eight months into my tour. He was smart, even-tempered, astute in his profession, and a true gentleman. He was influential in setting *Arleigh Burke* up for every inspection and certification wicket that laid the foundation for our intermediate and advanced underway training. He fully supported every vision I had for the ship and was superb in every way.

My second XO, the one with whom I deployed, was Lieutenant Commander John Dorey. John had an interesting background. I remember reading his professional biography prior to his arrival and being very impressed. Normally I didn't put much stock in a person's biography, because some people could make going to the grocery store sound like a lifetime achievement, but John's seemed unintentionally impressive. With the exception of attending the Naval Postgraduate School for eighteen months, John had spent his entire career on sea duty, and he was consistently recognized as the best junior officer in each of those commands. Even at the Surface Warfare Officer School, he finished number one in his class. John was smart and experienced, and as I learned shortly after he arrived, he was also tireless and relentless. Had I been a little insecure about my shortcomings, I may have been a bit intimidated or even threatened by him.

To anyone who knew both me and John, we probably couldn't have seemed more different or incompatible, but he and I got along perfectly. I know he represented and supported my priorities clearly to the department heads and the rest of the ship, and it wasn't long after he reported that I felt comfortable with him running the ship if I was away tending to something else.

John was very capable and confident, so life on the bridge of *Arleigh Burke* was calm—no matter the situation. John and I always seemed to be perfectly in sync on the bridge. Having spent so much time there throughout my career and especially as an XO, I was exacting in how I wanted people to drive the ship, talk on the radio telephone, craft their reports to me, and execute every task that originated in the pilot house. John had those same expectations and demands on the bridge, which made every special evolution go smoothly.

∽

Our southbound transit of the Suez Canal was the first for a destroyer since the attack on *Cole* a few months earlier. Thus, the attention and security surrounding our transit was understandably heightened. Even though higher authority had to approve the overall plan for the transit, some details were left strictly up to me depending on the situation. The trip typically takes about sixteen hours from start to finish (counting the time it takes to get clear of heavy traffic at Port Suez), but it's not a difficult one once you get inside the canal entrance.

From there we had about another nine days until we pulled into Bahrain for our operational briefings and introduction into the operations we would be supporting during the next few months. That transit was actually very pleasant. The weather was warm and the seas were mostly calm, and that made the underway replenishment with the Royal Fleet Auxiliary *Orangeleaf* on January 8 one of the more relaxing ones I had while in command.

My last few months brought me even closer to the crew. Our missions were the most intense and challenging of my career. The days and nights often consisted of non-stop action and were demanding for everyone on board. As is so common, those tough times really served to reveal what kind of team we had become, and it pulled us closer than ever before. With so many missions going on simultaneously, everyone had to fill in and often do things far beyond their specialties. Even if someone wasn't on a specific watch bill, that person still had to fill in behind someone else who was. I can recall standing on the bridge wing early one morning and watching about a dozen of my guys come back aboard after a fourteen-hour shift off the ship in some pretty harsh conditions. They were laughing and joking with the guys on the boat deck and were not the least bit short-tempered. I felt like a proud parent watching them come back aboard.

The daily routine for John and me had us on the bridge for at least eighteen hours. At night, when our operations intensified, we both stayed there until roughly 4:15 a.m., at which time John would go to his stateroom to shower and grab about two hours of sleep. Then at 6:30 a.m., John would return to the bridge and take over, while I went to my cabin, showered, and slept until 8:45 a.m. Opening the door to my cabin was the signal to my cook I was up and ready for coffee.

By then the ship was clear of the restricted waters in which we had been operating, so John would leave the bridge to join me in my cabin, where we would have our coffee and talk about the night's activities. It reminded me of the Friday afternoon routine Rob and I had had at BUD/S when we would end each week by having a few beers in our room.

CHAPTER TWENTY-TWO

My Best Day

It was on one of those mornings after a long night, as I was standing with my command master chief and John on the bridge wing, that I decided I was going to make sure everyone on the ship was recognized for their dedication and hard work. For as long as I had been in the navy, personal recognition had always been a source of some angst for many sailors. People seemed to view others as less deserving of the recognition, and I knew from doing zone inspections every week and reading the command climate surveys that *Arleigh Burke* was no different. I told John and the CMC I wanted them to meet with the officers and chief petty officers and find out if anyone on the ship was not carrying their weight, because I intended to award all deserving crewmembers (except for John and the CMC) Navy and Marine Corps Achievement Medals for their performances during the workups and deployment. I told them not to reveal the reason for their inquiries, as I wanted the event to be a surprise.

After a day or so, John and the CMC came to me and said that only two people on the ship had been identified as below-average performers, and their recommendation was that everyone except those two receive the award. We were in the middle of an intense, two-week operation in the Northern Arabian Gulf (NAG), and my plan was to have a no-notice awards ceremony after our last night in the NAG as we headed south to Manama, Bahrain.

John was an extremely gifted writer, so he quickly wrote citations for the different functions and roles the officers and crewmembers were executing. My administration department then secretly typed up citations for everyone on the ship except the two underperformers. I found that because I treated my crew in a manner that demonstrated trust, they never broke that trust. I never kept things from them unless it was something compartmentalized that I was bound not to disclose for security reasons. Asking them to keep this quiet was something I knew they would do. Even with the Internet being available on the ship, not a single person ever shared anything I asked be kept private.

My administrative team knocked out the 310 citations within only a few days, and on January 26, 2001, as we headed for Bahrain, I had the word passed on the ship's general announcing system for the two people who were not being recognized to come to my cabin and for the remainder of the crew to assemble on the flight deck.

When the two sailors came to my cabin, I had them come in and sit down. I told them what was about to happen and why they were not going to be part of it. I told them that if their performances improved, they would be reconsidered for the awards after deployment, but for now I expected them to do better.

Walking back to the fantail and seeing my crew there gave me a feeling of such pride. Most looked pretty tired, but all looked as if they were ready to do even more if that was what I was there to ask. It was another incredible moment I was fortunate to share with such a special group. I explained what was about to happen, and I told them not to judge whether the people behind, beside, or in front of them deserved the award. They should only assess whether they deserved it. If they determined they didn't deserve recognition, they had my support to step out of formation. Not a soul moved. I couldn't possibly describe their expressions in a way that would adequately reflect what they held. I could have spent forever shaking each person's hand and pinning the awards on their coveralls. It was the closest I had ever felt to my crew.

A short while later, when *Arleigh Burke* was sitting pier side in Bahrain, John came to my cabin and said he had received an email from the chief staff officer of our destroyer squadron who was in the Mediterranean Sea. The chief staff officer said that the commodore (my immediate boss) had caught wind of our awards ceremony and had asked if it was true I had given everyone on the ship a Navy Achievement Medal. Without consulting me before he replied, John sent a short email back that simply said, "Nope. Two shitheads didn't get them." I never heard another word about it, nor did I ever initiate contact with my commodore to discuss it. No one knew the efforts of my crew better than I did, and I was prepared to defend whatever actions I had taken to recognize those efforts.

I completely understood the perception that what I had done cheapened the award, but someone else's opinion didn't concern me. If someone really wanted to argue that point with me, I would have told that person to be concerned with their own awards and not what I did for my people. I never actually understood why awards mattered at all. I had instructors at BUD/S who didn't wear Purple Hearts they had been awarded because they believed the people who had inflicted their wounds should have been the ones receiving awards—not them. I believed that if a person's focus was on serving their people, why should recognition matter? That said, I did care about my guys, and I wanted to give them every advantage when it came time for advancement, and those Navy Achievement Medals would benefit them at some point.

As my tour neared its end, I spent increasingly more time thinking back to my life growing up in Pennsylvania. I had been blessed more than I could have ever imagined and certainly more than I thought I deserved. I had been given the privilege to serve at sea with a group of young people who never asked for more than what they had and were always willing to do more. Had I not known better, I would have thought they were all from Lancaster County, Pennsylvania.

As my final day aboard *Arleigh Burke* approached, I began to distance myself from those with whom I had become closest. I was both intentionally and subconsciously avoiding the subject of how much I was going to miss them. By the time I walked to the dais for my change of command ceremony, I had no idea how I would ever be able to express my gratitude for everything they had done for me. It was so much more than I could have ever done for them.

When my strike group commander finished his remarks, and I was introduced for the last time as the commanding officer of USS *Arleigh Burke*, I was just making my way back from places miles and years away from where I was now. Although I had some regrets, not a single one was because I had betrayed my commitment to my personal standards or my belief in the standards of conduct I had long held dear and absolute. I came back from that mental journey to the Quarryville store just in time to hear my boss's final words and with just enough time to collect my emotions before I stepped up to the microphone to say my good-byes.

Those next fifteen minutes saying good-bye were the absolute saddest of my life—far sadder than any loss in my life to that point. But, unlike those other losses, this one came with some regret. Regret for every night at sea that I went to bed without stopping by the galley to talk with my night baker. Regret for keeping unspoken my thoughts of someone's job well done or for being too pointed in my criticism during a zone inspection. I even had regret for sometimes assuming the worst in people rather than defaulting to the opposite. Every possible oversight in how I treated those I professed to care so much about weighed on me like an anchor.

With the exception of my closing remarks regarding my boss and his staff, and my relief, I spent every word during those fifteen minutes saying aloud those private thoughts of admiration that had gone unsaid. I told my night baker, a self-proclaimed *Star Trek* groupie, how much I enjoyed it when he asked me questions such as, "Would you characterize your leadership style as more like Captain Picard or Captain Kirk?" I told my small boat coxswain and rescue swimmer how much I enjoyed our nighttime boat rides in the Arabian Gulf. Their helmets were stenciled *Boss Man* and *Beef Cake*. *Boss Man* because the coxswain was in charge of the boat, and *Beef Cake* because my rescue swimmer had once worked as a Chippendale dancer before joining the navy and was very well-built, if I do say so myself. Life was never better than cruising with them on the smooth waters of the Arabian Gulf at night and seeing *Arleigh Burke* silhouetted by the moonlight. Some nights I would have them turn the engine off so we could just drift in the water near the transom, allowing me more time to appreciate the moment. The urge to dive into the water was almost uncontrollable, as it reminded me so much of my time at night on the water with my sister and grandfather.

I revealed to the crew how I would stand on the bridge wing, high above the pier, watching them reunite with their families after an underway period and feeling so blessed to have been at least partially responsible for that happy reunion. I laughed as I told them of all the times I would watch them interact on the foc'sle (forecastle) from my chair on the bridge during sea and anchor detail, and how funny it was to see one of my boatswain's mate petty officers "sizing people up." This BM3 had a piece of string roughly eighteen inches long that he would extend vertically in front of his shipmates, just "sizing them up." I could have gone on for hours sharing with them all the things they did that came to hold meaning for me, but I knew I couldn't hold on to that moment forever. Standing there, saying good-bye, I finally realized why so many captains seem to drone on forever at their change of command, knowing now it was because it was the last time they would ever be able to address their crew, and they didn't want that moment to end. By the time I finished my remarks and read my detaching orders, I was exhausted from wrestling to keep my emotions in check.

Later that night, I boarded a plane in Bahrain to begin my long flight home. As the wheels lifted off the runway, I again thought back in time. This time I remembered my first day aboard the *Pharris*. I passed many hours of that flight home thinking about the people who had made my tour on *Arleigh Burke* possible, and also wondering how in the world following my own code hadn't derailed that opportunity one of the many times it probably should have. For as much as I was going to miss my shipmates on *Arleigh Burke*, there was some relief that I hadn't screwed it up. I had finished the race, stayed true to myself, and made some great friends along the way.

Part V

My View from the Bridge Wing

"All truth passes through three stages. First, it is ridiculed. Second, it is violently opposed. Third, it is accepted as being self-evident."

– Arthur Schopenhauer

CHAPTER TWENTY-THREE

DUTY AND PERSONAL RESPONSIBILITY

One of the mantras I tired of hearing during my career was "Our people are our top priority." It didn't matter who the senior officer was; whenever they had an opportunity to address an assembled group, those were among the first words uttered. Yet from my perspective, many leaders' actions didn't support that mantra. I don't doubt they wanted that to be true; they just never saw the connection between caring leadership and results.

As I matured and approached command at sea, I spent time thinking long and hard about what it meant to take care of my people and be the type of leader I wanted to be for them. What were the boundaries of my duty toward them? Was I only responsible for them while we were on the ship during the day? Did my duty extend to every minute of the day? Should it concern their personal lives? Just what did it mean to truly care about my people? I also thought a great deal about what I deemed my responsibility to share with my officers and crew the moral perspectives I had gained over time. Among those were my perspectives on alcohol, pornography, and suicide—all things that can damage or destroy individual lives and undermine the success of an organization.

Alcohol

Over the course of our lives, most of us experience at least one moment when something that should have been evident from the beginning finally stops us in our tracks—a moment when we are blindsided by the obvious. Typically, these are moments of clarity, causing us to wonder how we failed to grasp the truth for so long.

For me, one such moment came when I was the commissioning executive officer of the *John S. McCain*. Even though I had experienced the death of a close childhood friend in a drunk driving accident, and had been arrested myself for drunk driving, it wasn't until my tour on *McCain* that I began to recognize the reach and impact of irresponsible drinking.

The incident that truly began to change my perspective on alcohol occurred on a Friday evening when one of our sailors was shot in the head outside of a San Diego nightclub. I had been in the navy for thirteen years at that point, and never had anyone in any of my previous commands suggested my consumption of alcohol be limited on my off-duty hours—except perhaps during a liberty brief overseas, and certainly never in connection to my responsibilities to my men.

Over the rest of my XO tour on *John S. McCain* after our sailor died, I began to formulate how I would approach the topic of alcohol consumption if I ever made it into command. For me, it was clear: I shouldn't drink at all in command or for the remainder of my career, because people depended on my ability to support them at any hour. I thought back on all those times as a junior officer when I would go on liberty (shore leave in an overseas port of call) or out on the town in homeport without any thought of what I would do if one of my chiefs called me and needed my support for one of our sailors. I felt like such a hypocrite. I had always thought I cared about my people, but I knew right then and there that my willingness to get drunk undermined that commitment.

In addition to the instance on *John S. McCain*, there was another situation while I was stationed at the Naval Academy when I was thankful I did not drink alcohol. That time came early on a Sunday morning when I was summoned to identify the body of a young man who had fallen from the window of his upper-story room at the academy. As I walked to the area where the body was located, I passed his two roommates, who were justifiably inconsolable. After seeing the body, I walked back to his roommates and stood with them for a few minutes before addressing where we were to go next. I cannot imagine having been there while hungover from a night of drinking.

Later I represented the Naval Academy at the services for the midshipman in his hometown. Anyone who has served in this capacity will tell you it's an experience like no other. When parents want and deserve answers to questions for which there are no suitable or acceptable answers, the senior person who represents the establishment where their child died has the potential to become the lightning rod for every ounce of their anger and resentment. I remember preparing myself for that possibility as I drove to the midshipman's hometown; however, the parents and entire family of my midshipman could not have been more gracious. Their kindness in the midst of their grief demonstrated how truly special they were.

For much of my time driving to and from the funeral, I went over in my mind what could be learned from this tragedy. I don't know whether it was ever determined that alcohol was a factor in my midshipman's fall, but I suspect it was.

Upon my return to the academy, I brought the six hundred midshipmen in my battalion together and explained that during the upcoming home football games, I would not be approving alcohol for the tailgaters because I wanted them to know what it was like to attend a social function without being allowed to drink. I asked that they give me one hour of their time at the tailgate party, and after that, if they were of legal drinking age and wanted to attend an event with alcohol, they were free to do so. My point was that at some time during their military careers, they would likely attend a social event where, because of an upcoming mission, they would not be allowed to consume alcohol, and I wanted them to experience what that was like before that time. I knew from my own experience that some people grow up in environments where they never consider not drinking alcohol once of age—or even in the years leading up to that point. I wanted them to experience that option now. I asked them to consider how they would respond once they were commissioned if they ever had to respond to a call like the one I'd received about their fellow midshipman.

The midshipmen seemed to take the decision in stride. A few even stopped by my office on the Monday mornings following the games to tell me it wasn't as tough as they thought it would be. Every step of the way, I explained my reasons for my decision, and I updated them every week on when the trial would likely end. I told them it was not permanent and wouldn't even extend much past the football season's midpoint. I don't know if this changed any of the midshipmen's drinking habits, but I do know it gave them something they might later fall back on.

∽

During both my command tours, I told my wardroom what my expectations were for them regarding their consumption of alcohol, and that if they had an issue with it, they needed to let me know right then. That way it would be clear to their departments or divisions who not to call in the event someone needed after-hours support. My boss once approached me about this policy. When he asked me how I planned to enforce my standard regarding alcohol, I quickly replied that I wasn't going to enforce it. It was up to my officers to decide whether they thought my expectations were unreasonable.

Would I take those who fell short to captain's mast? No. Would they read about it in their fitness reports? No. I knew the playing field I put them on was inconsistent with their peers', but I wanted them to start thinking about the impact of alcohol on their duties and responsibilities to their fellow shipmates.

I also understood from my own experiences that making mistakes and figuring out the acceptable bounds of behavior is part of self-discovery. My belief in an officer's obligation to duty was different, and although it wasn't the same for an ensign as it was for a lieutenant commander department head, I felt a genuine obligation to help those younger officers progress positively through their self-discovery regarding the use of alcohol, without it having a permanent negative impact on their young careers.

As I talked with the officers about my alcohol policy, I asked them to think about how many times they had heard a leader say people were our number-one resource and as such had to be our number-one concern—apart from completing the mission. I knew that in an organization where lives depend on decisions, nothing should be more important than completing the task, but also at the top of the list should be a genuine concern for how to get the job done. I expressed to my officers my expectations for their responsible use of alcohol—that its consumption must never prevent them from being able to support their people. My message was that no matter the circumstances, sailors should be able to call them any time of the day or night and ask for help. I challenged each of them to find a strategy that would work for and make sense to them.

I asked them all to consider how much they truly cared about their people and what they were willing to do for them. Even though I had never met officers who admitted to having limits to what they were willing to do for their people, I knew in many cases, there are limits. These limits typically aren't what you would expect them to be, and always seem to reside in the leader's own lack of self-discipline or foresight. Somehow, many officers do not see the connection between the consumption of alcohol and its impact on being able to fully support the needs of their people. Giving up alcohol or limiting its consumption should be easy—especially when being able to support people is the motivation.

I elected not to extend the same expectations to my crew, not because I didn't believe in their obligation to honor their duty, but because I knew that due to their age and inexperience, many would fall short, and I didn't want alcohol to be the ship's main focus.

∽

From the instant I had my epiphany about alcohol back on *McCain*, my own drinking habits started to change. It was odd to think how casually I had approached drinking all those years before. Looking back, I recalled how unnatural it would have felt to be at a party and not be holding a beer. It was as if I wouldn't know what to do with my hands. I imagine that's why some people find quitting smoking so difficult. For some reason, though, I naturally fell back on my experiences as a young man, and before going to a party, I would mentally prepare myself for the fact that I wasn't going to drink. It took me back to running cross-country in college: I would always check our practice schedules hours in advance so that I could mentally prepare myself for the agony of the days when we ran intervals. I couldn't just waltz into those workouts unprepared and expect to breeze through; I needed to build my resolve ahead of time. That became the approach I took to not drinking at parties, and I was amazed at how easy it was to transition from being a drinker to a nondrinker.

∽

I remember a very close friend once phoning me about his concern regarding a mutual friend's drinking habits. I had known of the issue for years and twice had approached our friend about my concerns. Unfortunately it did nothing but hurt our relationship, and I finally gave up. I knew this was a time in his life when he had to find out for himself what he wanted and what he was willing to do to get it. Because Rick and the friend who phoned me were about to go on their annual winter hunting trip to Canada, I suggested during that call that when they get to Canada, they forego their traditional stop to stock up on local beer for the week. I will never forget my friend groaning on the phone and saying, "I don't think I can do that."

"Well," I replied, "then don't tell me again how much you care about Rick if you aren't willing to sacrifice one week's worth of drinking for him."

It was the last time he ever spoke of the issue with me.

∞

I would like to think that all organizations do what they can to encourage people to drink more responsibly, but I believe we need to approach the irresponsible use of alcohol in a manner that directly ties our sobriety to our duty and responsibility not only as leaders, but as parents, friends, and citizens. To me, that connection is irrefutable. Even if we never reach the goal of having zero alcohol-related incidents, at least that number will be markedly fewer.

Pornography, Sexual Assault, and Misconduct

It goes without saying that a good leader will strive to minimize suffering to the best of his or her ability, and that he or she will demand a standard of behavior from their officers and crew consistent with that intent. However, the lens through which we view our sphere of influence is often narrow when it comes to suffering. This is especially true if the path between one's actions and the suffering of another is distant or diffuse.

The act of exploitation almost always leads to suffering. Yet the world's sex industry—the roots of which lie in exploitation—is reported to be in excess of $98 billion annually and growing. Sex traffickers, brothel owners, participants in the insidious world of child pornography—we righteously condemn such players. But even the passive enjoyment of adult pornography fuels demand in an inherently exploitative industry, no matter our attempts to rationalize and justify our consumption. As a leader in a predominantly male culture that historically permits and even glamorizes the sexual appetites of sailors as they extend to the consumption of adult magazines, pornography, and live adult entertainment, I could not ignore the ramifications of this mindset. Its effects on the supply chain and on the ship's atmosphere, especially with regard to respect toward female sailors, disturbed me deeply.

As the commanding officer of a ship, there were countless directives that guided my actions, and outlined my duties and responsibilities. Among those was United States Navy Regulations. Chapter eight, article 820 stipulates, "The Commanding Officers shall: use all proper means to foster high morale, and to develop and strengthen the moral and spiritual well-being of the personnel under his or her command."

I read that to mean that I, as the commanding officer, was well within my bounds to do whatever I felt was necessary to promote the moral behavior of those in my command. I was expected to know how to do that. I didn't need clarification from my boss to know what to do. So after I talked about the responsible use of alcohol with my officers on *Arleigh Burke*, I jumped straight into my view on pornography. Only on this subject, my thoughts and expectations for their behavior and conduct extended to the entire crew.

I think it's a cop-out when leaders hide behind the line that they won't legislate morals. Every time I've heard a commanding officer say that, I've wanted to ask, "Why not? Parents and churches do it all the time."

I couldn't have cared less what anyone's religious views were—or whether they had any at all. I only cared about the character of the people under my charge and the manner in which they exercised their responsibilities as leaders, and as members of the United States Navy.

As a service, we mandate what tattoos are acceptable, both in content and body location. We enforce a zero tolerance for drugs, even while marijuana is legal in some states. We limit the number of earrings someone can wear, the length of one's hair, and even its style. We dictate uniform standards right down to the style of undershirts. Yet we shy away from setting a standard for human conduct and decency, even though we acknowledge that our people's conduct and behavior is expected to represent only the highest standards. We do have a policy and process for dealing with sexual harassment and misconduct, but we never tell our sailors to stay out of strip clubs or other establishments that overtly condone subjugating others, unless it just happens to be a location on the "off-limits" list.

I have been continually amazed at the male point of view when it comes to pornography. Most men openly admit to enjoying pornography in some form without the slightest bit of embarrassment. It's as if men believe it's an inalienable human right, and that enjoying pornography is a requirement for "real" manhood that should be accepted by all.

I recognize pornography as something that subjugates, objectifies, and devalues another human being. It represents a culture where the *haves* exploit the *have-nots*, and that is not a culture I want to be part of. The overt enjoyment of and participation in forms of pornography clearly don't create an environment conducive to making everyone feel like an equally important member of the team.

Whether we want to admit it or not, there is a clear double standard in how we (Americans) view men and women. Catcalls and jocular, lewd comments about women are seen as normal male behavior, a form of male bonding even, and women are often expected to tolerate them as such. Yet most men (and even other women) would be taken aback if a woman behaved similarly in her observation of male bodies. The implicit message is that, sexually speaking, men are the consumers, and women are there to be consumed, whether they like it or not.

∽

Not until well into my naval career did I ever hear the subject of pornography addressed. At best it was ignored, and at worst it was encouraged and glamorized. "Porn lockers," as they were referred to, once existed on every ship. Typically, they had a collection of magazines and videos the officers and chiefs could borrow for their personal viewing. About the time mixed-gender crews became the norm on surface combatants, a policy was put in place to ban pornography aboard ships, but its enforcement was often spotty, in my experience. If ever a policy was "don't ask, don't tell," it was this one.

But the conduct of sailors going to strip clubs ashore was never addressed, and it was certainly never addressed as something that might create an uncomfortable atmosphere for the female officers and crew, who invariably knew how their male shipmates passed their time while on liberty.

The military as a whole repeatedly speaks of its commitment to eliminating sexual assaults from within its ranks, yet there is much more we could do. Most obvious would be to prohibit participation in activities that objectify women. Just as the navy doesn't *demand* responsible drinking—even though many sexual assaults occur after or during excessive or irresponsible alcohol use—we don't widely enforce a moral code that U.S. Navy Regulations state is a commanding officer's obligation to uphold.

I would be shocked if every year the Chief of Naval Operations (CNO) didn't gather all his newly selected flag officers and challenge them to be bold, to lead from the front, and to have the courage to take actions that would lead to positive and needed change. Does anyone expect to ever hear the CNO or chairman of the Joint Chiefs of Staff say that we, as the armed services, have reached an acceptable level of sexual assault or misconduct? I don't. So why don't we do more than tell our leaders to be bold? Let's demand that newly selected flag and general officers go after the irresponsible use of alcohol and the plague of sexual assault. If we don't give these internal enemies the same priority we give those overseas that threaten our country and our values, over time they could become even more detrimental than another foreign attack on our soil.

For me, to either openly or tacitly allow your officers and crew to enjoy a practice or activity that subjugates another human being is absolutely incongruent with the navy's expressed commitment to eliminating sexual harassment and misconduct. But throughout my career, I've had senior officers hide behind a reluctance to legislate morals, or a fear of coming across as forcing their religious beliefs on others.

As evidenced by the "above the fold" reporting of incidents involving members of the military, the general civilian population and the media seem to hold those in the U.S. military to a higher standard than the average citizen. So why shouldn't the military take the lead in changing this culture and demand a level of moral decency that discourages any activity that contributes to or condones sexual exploitation?

Likewise, individuals in leadership positions must walk the walk. When leaders don't represent the best of all characteristics, it prevents organizations from ever truly becoming the best they can be. It limits how much people are willing to do for others, and it certainly shows those in the organization what the leader is unwilling to do to make everyone feel like a valued team member.

∽

Even taking sexual exploitation out of the conversation, women in many occupations often face an uneven playing field when it comes to simply being able to work in an environment that supports doing their job. I believe every person, man or woman, should have the same chance for success. They should be afforded the same environment and working conditions to fully support their advancement. Unfortunately, this is frequently not the case. In my experience, women are often at a disadvantage because of the way men behave around them.

This was evident to me when I was stationed aboard the *John S. McCain* as the executive officer. Near the end of the ship's construction period in Bath, Maine, the crew was moved aboard while final preparations were made for the ship's turnover from the shipyard to the navy. During that time, shipyard workers and *McCain*'s crew worked side by side to finish the construction.

As with every ship on which I served, *McCain* had an all-male crew, so the only women working on the ship were employees of Bath Iron Works. Over the first few days of that turnover period, work was being done in the overhead of the passageway directly outside my stateroom door. The space where the work was being done was relatively confined, and with a ladder in the passageway, it was difficult for anyone to traverse that area.

For the first two days, a female shipyard worker accomplished the work. Almost non-stop throughout those two days, at least one of the men of the *McCain* crew would be outside my door talking to her. I don't know how she got her job done. I repeatedly had to remind the men to keep moving and allow the worker to do her job without distraction.

On the third day, the woman was gone; however, the work continued. Only now, a male shipyard worker conducted it. The most I heard spoken to him was when a crewmember asked him to move so he could pass. I thought about how tough it must have been every single day for that woman to do her job—not to mention the dilemma she had in deciding how to get the men to leave her alone. If she protested the attention, I'm sure she would have been labeled as something unbecoming, and if she entertained the attention, she risked being labeled something equally unflattering.

I used this example as a way to illustrate to my officers behavior that detracts from the workplace and that serves no purpose but to alienate or isolate a section of the team. Men who openly engage in activities that degrade or objectify women are obstacles to creating the type of environment I demanded on *Arleigh Burke*.

Ultimately, though, as individuals, we all have to sit down and ask ourselves whether our behavior promotes unity of command, camaraderie, and true teamwork, and, also, whether it projects an honorable image of our people and our work. I guarantee you when someone walks up to a member of the armed services on the street, in an airport, or anywhere else, and thanks them for serving our country, that person would think twice if that same service member were walking out of a strip club or buying an adult magazine at a newsstand.

As I told my officers what I expected their conduct to be at all times, I acknowledged it would put them at a disadvantage with their peers to hold them to a standard so far beyond what their contemporaries were expected to uphold. I did not, therefore, discipline them under the Uniform Code of Military Justice when they fell short of my standard. However, falling short of my expectations on this matter did influence how I graded them on their performance reviews, because I was not going to endorse an officer who thought it was acceptable to objectify another human being, only to have that person later serve in command. I didn't go out of my way to know what my officers did ashore or in homeport during their time off, but if they made it my business, I did not ignore it.

Even though the media still promotes an idealized vision of what an officer should be, somewhere along the way, the military seems to have lost sight of that ideal. In my experience, the model of what was acceptable on a given ship was essentially up to the standards of my commanding officer, and even then there seemed to be a lack of concern so long as nobody got in trouble. When I sat down with my wardroom on *Arleigh Burke*, I'm sure it was the first time anyone had addressed moral conduct with them in these words.

I ended my discussion on pornography, strip clubs, and related activities by asking my officers to consider the environment in which they would want their wives or daughters to work and then to consider what it would be like if the roles were reversed—with men being viewed and treated as if they were less significant. I also asked them to consider the impact of their actions on the sex industry's growth and if they wanted to be a part of making the world better. By the time I finished my thoughts on alcohol and pornography, I could tell some of them—especially the department heads—needed some time to digest everything I'd said. That was a good start. I wanted them to really think about their own personal codes of conduct, and what they wanted them to be.

Emotional Duress and Suicide

A huge part of caring for your people is creating an environment in which you truly get to know them. Getting to know them should allow you to better recognize when they aren't themselves. And when you care about your people and recognize a change in their usual demeanor, at a minimum, you end up mentioning it and trying in some way to lift their spirits.

Although I had seen on *John S. McCain* the impact one person can make on a ship's atmosphere, it wasn't until my time on *Arleigh Burke* that I realized just how much people are aware of the captain's actions and mood.

I have always enjoyed music. I like how certain songs have a way of sending me back to times in my past—mostly to times that hold a great deal of meaning for me. One morning as I drove to the ship, I heard a song from the movie *Stealing Home,* which had been one of my first wife's favorite movies. It immediately brought back fun memories of my time with her. She had died a few years earlier in a car accident, so I was unusually subdued as I walked across the quarterdeck that morning. Normally I would have something to say in passing with the watch officer, but on this day I simply saluted, said good morning, and went straight to my cabin without another word. Within a minute of walking into my cabin, my wardroom cook came to me and asked if I was okay. He said the quarterdeck had called him to say it seemed as if I had something on my mind, and he wanted to make sure I was all right. At that moment I realized how much the crew cared for me, and it made me want to serve them even more. It also told me how in tune they were with my moods and demeanor, and I would need to be careful not to convey something unintentional to them. That act of kindness from my cook immediately brought me out of my mood and taught me a great deal about how even the smallest-seeming gesture can have a meaningful impact. I used that kind gesture as a reminder to pay the same attention to the moods of my crew.

It's natural to allow the conditions and responsibilities in our lives to put us on edge. Certainly given the environments in which many of us work, stress is inevitable. I realize some of the situations in which people find themselves truly are life-and-death, but I also know that it is often during those life-and-death situations that people find the most clarity. Maybe it's because those times give us less opportunity for idle thoughts or over-thinking things. Whatever the reasons, it's often the mundane, or the slow build-up of seemingly small issues, that can push us nearer the edge.

A few years ago, a senior officer I knew committed suicide. Although I only knew him from the few times he brought his command to our building for training, his genuine kindness had always impressed me. He appeared comfortable with what he knew and what he didn't know, and he always seemed to interact professionally with his staff.

One day soon after his suicide, a colleague of mine commented in passing that he couldn't begin to understand how anyone could reach the point in their life where they would take that final measure. It was all I could do not to punch him. How could anyone spend thirty years in the navy, as this man had, and be so out of touch with the stress of the profession—not to mention life's everyday stresses?

I believe that each of us has emotional vulnerabilities which, when exposed, have the potential to drive us to our breaking points. It's that unknown vulnerability that none of us ever know exists until we are reeling from it. Fortunately, many people never have to face it head-on. But I believe it exists for everyone.

As leaders we have to appreciate that just as bodies can live with certain dormant viruses for years (or forever), so too can people function perfectly without knowing the grim reality that somewhere deep in their psyche resides the potential for suicide.

I found that place in 2010. Having endured my share of challenging human losses, plus my experience at BUD/S, I honestly believed the potential for suicide did not exist in me. I can say now with all sincerity, though, that if not for knowing what the act would do to my children and mother, and the timely help of friends who recognized that look in my eyes, I very likely would have taken that final step. I thought I knew everything there was to know about myself, but clearly this one major vulnerability had gone unrevealed until that point.

I would never say my losses come close to the losses and hardships many have endured, but I've had my share. The event that truly revealed this vulnerability in me was my separation and divorce from my wife of twenty years. More accurately, it was the dissolution of my family and the loss of the home I had shared with my three children that took me to that ominous place. It was the loss of the place where I had found comfort after time at sea or a long day, and when it was gone, its absence was far more devastating than I could have ever imagined.

For someone who had always put others first, taking the step to seek a better life left me with enormous guilt for breaking up my family. There was no infidelity. My marriage had just descended to a point where I felt nothing could be worse, and it would be better for everyone if my wife and I finally let each other go.

Let me say to anyone who believes there is a better or a right time for ending a marriage: rethink that. Divorce is never easy—especially when children of any age are involved. For me the selfishness of needing something much more fulfilling was devastating. Had I known how hard giving up that life was going to be, I doubt I would have had the courage to do it.

I had never before experienced emotional turmoil beyond some slight rational anxiety before facing something uncertain, but when separated from my family, severe anxiety took hold of me without warning. I would often wake in the middle of the night and just lie in bed moaning. I was nearly debilitated.

In order to make it to work on time, I would have to get up by 2:30 or 3:00 a.m, taking the process of getting ready one painful step at a time, until I was out the door and on my way. It took every ounce of mental strength I had to get from the bed to my couch, where I would then have to lie for about an hour. From there I'd muster just enough energy to make it to the bathroom to shave. Showering and dressing took even more strength.

What made the anxiety even worse was that I felt powerless against it, and it could strike without warning. Other times, when I could sense its approach, it felt like a freight train coming. And when that feeling came, I had to move fast to get out of the office or back to my apartment before it overwhelmed me. I had been sad before, but this was so foreign to me it felt as though I had been transported into someone else's body—someone I didn't recognize. It was the most horribly confusing and frightening feeling I have ever known.

Weekends became almost unbearable because of my extra free time, and if I stayed in Virginia Beach, I made sure to keep myself as busy as possible to keep my mind off my personal life. Fortunately, a good friend, Bill Garland, invited me to start working out with him at the Oceana gym first thing every Saturday morning. On Sunday mornings I'd go to Mass and then that night to a divorce care group meeting at the church. Otherwise I went to my mother's in Pennsylvania every weekend.

My friend and supervisor, Chuck Kennard, extended an open invitation for dinner every night at his home that also helped me immeasurably. Sharing dinner with Chuck, his daughter, Amanda, and her husband, Stu, was sometimes my only escape during my weekday evenings.

When trout season opened in Pennsylvania, I went home every single weekend, trying to find some solace along the streams I had fished since I was a kid, but even that didn't help. Finally, in the middle of the night during one of my visits to Mom's, I woke with anxiety that drove me to the brink of what I could take. My doctor had been so concerned that for weeks he had tried to convince me to take anti-depressants, but I refused, thinking they would turn me into someone even more remote and unfamiliar. I woke Mom up and said something just didn't feel right, and I feared I might take my life if I was alone. Mom jumped out of bed as fast as a seventy-nine-year-old woman could and sat with me in the den as we talked.

As only Maynard Colley's daughter could do, Mom told me enough was enough and that I was tougher than this. We got in the car around 1:00 a.m. and drove the mile to the cemetery where my father was buried. When we got to the cemetery, Mom said to get out of the car and go talk to Dad—alone. I walked down the path leading to Dad's grave between the headstones marking the graves of many people I had known growing up in Quarryville. The moon was so full that night, the headstones cast shadows on the ground, and I could easily find my way to the plot where all of Dad's family was buried. It reminded me of all those early mornings I had spent walking with Dad to our deer stands, guided only by moonlight.

By the time I reached Dad's grave, I was sobbing as never before. I sat down in front of his headstone engraved with a hunting scene and pleaded with Dad to give me the kick in the ass that only he could give. By then, I was three months into my emotional descent, and at six feet tall and 145 pounds, I had lost almost thirty pounds. Even though it had been twenty-seven years since I'd heard my father's voice, I swear I heard him say, "Come on, Al. You're better than this. Now get over it, and move on." (Dad always called me Al—never Alan. It was comforting hearing him call me that.)

Looking back, those words were the best thing he has ever done for me. Carrying my shotgun or consoling me with a hand on the shoulder all those years ago when I found that damn teepee were finally and forever displaced as his greatest demonstration of his love for me. For all that Dad could have said when he was alive and didn't, those few words more than made up for it. I stood, placed both hands on his headstone, and cried one last time. I thanked him and told him how much I missed him before walking back to the car. I knew the moment my hands left his headstone I was going to be all right. As suddenly as depression and anxiety had found me, they were gone just as fast. I'm not saying that this was the end of my bad days, but it was the end of my depression. Every day after that was better than the one before, and I never again felt the anxiety that had gripped me so tightly.

Despite how bad things got, I never once prayed for help. Just as I never asked for things as a kid, I didn't feel right asking God to help me out of a situation I had brought upon myself for seeking a happier life. I know our faith tells us to bring our troubles to whom we worship, but that has never been my way. Thankfully, He gave me a family and friends who made all the difference.

As leaders, we have to be as aware as possible of the emotional vulnerabilities in every person. History is full of examples of seemingly happy, successful people secretly harboring self-doubt that ultimately leads them to take their own lives. I also know that even with the benefit of 20/20 hindsight, it's impossible to always detect the signs that indicate those vulnerabilities. Leaders have to be aware of these very real possibilities and create environments in which people will be confident and secure enough to come forward when they find themselves approaching their emotional vulnerabilities.

CHAPTER TWENTY-FOUR

LEADERSHIP STYLES

When I addressed the subject of leadership with my officers, I began by relating leadership to my youth playing baseball. My father was good enough to play professionally, and having him as a coach, I knew some of the best hitters of all time looked incredibly unorthodox in the batter's box. In all my years playing and coaching baseball, I never heard anyone tell their players to hold the bat or stand in the batter's box like Rod Carew, Carl Yastrzemski, or Pete Rose, three hitters with some of the most awkward-looking batting stances in the game's history. Statistically, though, they are among the best hitters the game has ever seen.

As with batting stances and running styles, a person's most effective leadership style should be uniquely their own. However, just as there are certain imperatives for hitting a baseball, so too are there some imperatives for effective leadership. At the top of that list is genuinely caring more for your people than you do for yourself. I also believe leaders should care about how the people working for them view their leadership styles. I know this goes against *Leadership 101*; however, good leaders recognize the impact their styles have on the overall readiness of their commands, departments, divisions, and even work centers.

Inspirational leadership is what everyone deserves, but it is nearly impossible to achieve if the leader is disliked or even despised. In order to inspire people to perform their best, there has to be an element of their effort that is motivated by a desire to not let the leader down.

I told all my crewmembers that if their natural styles were abusive, defensive, or demeaning, that was far from what those we led deserved. I also told them I would not stand for it—no matter how much success they felt they achieved through their methods. I can guarantee you that for every person who has ever been on the front page of a newspaper for being fired for creating an abusive command climate, there were dozens (if not hundreds) who were not surprised. Yet every person who had the chance to document or do something about that abusive style never took action as long as the person was getting the job done.

I reminded my officers and crew of the enormous gratification they would feel if they were genuinely committed to unselfish forms of leadership. Everyone, whether officer or enlisted, deserves to be led and inspired only by those selfless enough to embrace that sacred position of leading. If those of us in positions of naval command genuinely care about the future of our organization, we must ensure our young officers are viewed and treated as if they are the future. When I evaluated my officers and crews, my assessment of their leadership was the most important aspect of those evaluations.

I have long observed how unfortunate it is when sailors perform admirably in spite of poor leadership rather than because of great leadership. Most sailors are professional enough to get the job done because of who they are—not because their leader inspires them. I'm certain that for the most selfish leaders, that fact is lost on them entirely. They embrace each success as a reflection of their leadership, which further validates their beliefs that their styles work. Results alone rarely tell the complete story of how they were achieved.

Knowing and being comfortable with who I was did not mean I was through making course corrections. Throughout even the latter years of my career, I made plenty of mistakes because I failed to regulate some of my own tendencies—more specifically, my bad ones. One such tendency was an intolerance for a less-than-cheerful approach to a hard day's work. When someone reacted to work in a way I perceived as reluctant or immature, I assumed that person had lived a pampered life and turned their hard day's work into a *really* hard day's work.

One problem with being the boss at any level is that most people won't confront you, because they either fear the repercussions or think it's unprofessional. For the really despised leaders, perhaps people don't approach them because they want them to fail. Because I never shied away from confronting my bosses, I assumed that if those people working in my division, department, or command had issues with me, they would do the same. This reflects my childhood belief that if I could do something, anyone could do it. I couldn't have been more wrong.

Never once in my career leading to my command of *Arleigh Burke* had I known any officer to be formally counseled for having an abusive leadership style, but I knew that if such a style existed on *Arleigh Burke*, it would change. I wouldn't accept it, and I was finally in a position that allowed me to reach across departmental lines to address such matters.

During one of my ship tours, I served with a few officers who I almost immediately knew were abusive. One of them would regularly take great pleasure in telling stories around the wardroom table about the demeaning, vile beratements a prior commanding officer had dished out. He told these stories with great reverence and respect for the man, and I was beginning to realize he was emulating this style on our ship. I endured these stories only a few times before inviting him to my cabin after lunch, where I told him never to speak the man's name again in my presence because I disapproved of such an abusive leadership style. I told this officer that when I evaluated his fitness for his next assignment, most of that evaluation would be based on my opinion of his ability to effectively lead people. I told him by treating people with the respect they deserve, they perform at their highest levels. That's the reason great leaders achieve unimaginable results.

∞

On my first day in command, I told my people that I expected to be notified if an abusive leadership style existed on our ship, even if it was mine. I had learned long before that how we view ourselves is not an accurate reflection of reality. There is how we see ourselves, and how others see us, which may well come closer to how we truly are.

One day during an underway period, one of my crewmembers came to my cabin to express his concern for one of our younger sailors. He told me this sailor's supervisor was being extremely abusive, and the sailor was having a tough go of things. The sailor's wife had recently given birth, so in addition to the stress of his job, weighing on him were family commitments he felt he wasn't able to adequately address. I went to the space where the young sailor was on watch. I put my hand on his shoulder and asked how he was doing. More specifically, I asked how he was enjoying the navy lifestyle. He hesitated for a moment before replying that it wasn't going as well as he would like. I told him to stop by my cabin after he finished his watch so we could relax for a moment and talk about things.

When he came by, I asked him how his supervisor treated him and his fellow divisional shipmates. He said his supervisor rarely communicated in a calm manner when addressing them, and the verbal beatings they often endured came in person and via email. Having served for years on ships without email, I found it odd to even consider communicating with someone within the same lifelines via that means—especially on a ship that was less than two football fields long and twenty yards wide. I asked this young man if he had saved any emails from his supervisor and, if he had, to provide me with a copy of one that was representative of all the emails. I didn't want to see the worst one. I wanted to see a typical email. What he brought to me was unbelievable. It was profane and threatening from its introduction, and it made me wonder about the emotional stability of the man who had written it.

I finished my meeting with the young man and had the supervisor come to my stateroom. After inviting him to come in and sit down, I handed him the email I had been provided and told him to read it—not aloud but just to himself. From his expression, I knew he recognized the email immediately and was genuinely embarrassed.

I did not go through this man's chain of command when I asked him to come to my cabin, because my intent was primarily to address and weed out negative leadership. I was more interested in stopping the behavior than trying to permanently damage his career. There would be plenty of opportunities for that if the behavior continued. For now, I wanted the counseling to remain private.

This supervisor's abusiveness was actually very surprising. He was a nice man—at least in my presence—and had been an above-average sailor in both his results and professional knowledge. He had even been a finalist for recognition as my top midgrade enlisted sailor. I told him I knew he could be a better leader than this and asked him what was going on. In the end he revealed quite a bit about pressures I had been unaware he was feeling.

The point is, if you truly care about leadership and how people are being led, you will strive to create an environment in which people will approach you with concerns and observations. If a complaint was just someone complaining without validity, I found out. I never went after someone based solely on an unsubstantiated claim.

If we truly want to eradicate negative leadership styles, we have to be willing to address them openly and honestly, and we have to give those who need some recalibration of their styles the attention and time they need to adjust. We can't just condemn abusive leaders. We need to give them the opportunity and guidance to change.

Just as some people have never considered that their drinking habits might warrant adjustment, so too are there people who have never been confronted about their leadership styles. And as they promote through the ranks, those styles are reinforced as both effective and desirable. With no reason to reflect on their methods, they'll continue to assume everything is fine and acceptable. When I confronted my boss at the Pentagon, he at least considered my opinion and then modified his style, and I believe he appreciated my honesty.

I finished my discussion on leadership styles by telling each officer that my number-one criterion when evaluating them was my assessment of whether or not I would want them leading my son or daughter.

CHAPTER TWENTY-FIVE

ATHLETICS AND LEADERSHIP

One of the highlights of my tour at the Naval Academy was my association with the academy's football team. At the Naval Academy, all sports teams, whether NCAA or club, have at least one active duty military member from the staff who serves as the representative for the midshipmen on that team. So, when I was asked to serve as the senior of the two officers assigned to support the football team, my job was to help resolve issues that prevented the players from fully participating. Conduct and academic issues were the most common situations that required my attention. In every one of those instances, I made finding a resolution that favored the midshipman's return to the team my number-one priority. I loved this role of serving the football players and the coaching staff, because serving them was as close to serving sailors as I could get on shore duty.

Although the academy football players weren't enjoying a great reputation within the brigade when I was first assigned to represent them, I found them to be exceptional young men who were grossly misrepresented by that reputation. Right from the start, I was impressed with their toughness, their selflessness, their commitment, and the love they had for one another. I had played sports my entire life, including wrestling, but I had never played organized football beyond the junior-high level. The physical pounding the academy players repeatedly absorbed was eye-opening to me. Being on the sidelines, I now had a front-row seat to that pounding, and it gave me a whole new perspective on what these young men were sacrificing. They weren't going to play professionally after college; they were going to serve their country in either the navy or the Marine Corps. They weren't motivated to play for anything more than the satisfaction they felt serving their school, their coaching staff, and each other.

Most of those players who commissioned into the navy would go on to serve aboard ships as surface warfare officers. Those who went into the Marine Corps usually just wanted whatever specialty would put them in the best position to lead men in battle. So in essence, these young men on the football team were the men who were going to be stepping into important leadership positions almost immediately after commissioning. If there was any single group of midshipmen at the Naval Academy more deserving of respect than these kids, I didn't know who that could be. As I got to know these young men individually, it made me feel good to know the quality of leadership our fleet sailors and Marines would be getting when they got a Naval Academy football player as their division officer or platoon leader.

The parallels between athletics and leadership are endless. Athletes, especially those on team sports, know that it takes a group effort to be successful. They appreciate the value of work done in the trenches or behind the scenes that enable the team, and at times individuals, to excel. For football players at the Naval Academy, they have to learn how to overcome defeat and physical suffering and how to compete against teams with bigger, faster, and stronger players. They know that winning doesn't come easy, that their margin for error is small, and that any lapse in their preparation and execution will likely result in a loss. What better parallel to leadership is there than that? The commitment and courage I saw these players display day after day made me strive even harder to do all I could to support them.

Unlike my college athletic experience, where after cross-country or track practice I studied for classes such as thanatology and *Math: An Everyday Experience*, every one of these young men at one point in their Naval Academy education had electrical engineering, quantitative methods, or differential equations classes they had to prepare for. And also unlike my college athletic experience, where I was free immediately after practice, these guys often had hours of treatment for injuries that further lengthened their days. Seeing the players do this without complaint was very inspiring.

Every time one of the players had to attend an academic performance board for receiving low grades, I stood in the proceedings as an advocate for him. At almost every academic board I attended in support of a football player, a member of the review board would ask him to decide whether it was more important to continue playing football or to give up playing in order to concentrate on his studies, ostensibly to better ensure his graduation. Before the player had a chance to answer that loaded question, I would interject that I didn't think it was a fair one. The board member was asking a lifelong athlete to give up on a more disciplined lifestyle for one that would just give him more free time. I understood the question; I just knew it came from someone who didn't share the same perspective and experience as the player. I also knew additional spare time didn't necessarily mean that the time would be spent on studies or even wisely.

From the day I had been assigned to represent the team, there were only two practices I didn't attend, and both were due to my need to attend conduct boards for midshipmen in the battalion for which I was responsible. Otherwise, I was on the field before every practice and stayed until most of the guys had left the locker room—so I got to know the team and coaches quite well. Out of the entire team of eighty or so young men, I only had an issue with one of them.

The young man I didn't get along with was one of our defensive linemen. I disliked everything about him, especially his attitude and the fact that he didn't think he needed to respond to a simple "good morning" when we passed. After only the second time he failed to return my greeting, I stopped him and told him to come see me in my office before going to practice that afternoon.

When he reported to my office, I invited him in, shut the door, and got right to the matter. I said, "Here's the deal, I don't like you, and I sense the feeling is mutual. So we are going to stay in this office until we figure out if our feelings are misguided, or if we each have some valid reasons for disliking the other."

I wasn't about to dress him down because he had complete disregard for basic military courtesy, or remind him how absolutely miserable I could make his life simply by virtue of our disparate positions in the academy food chain. At BUD/S I had learned the art of screwing with someone's life from the professionals, so I could have had some real fun following through had that been my chosen route. But I really wanted to understand his perspective, and I truly wanted to know if his feelings toward me had valid reasons.

I started by asking him why he refused to answer me when I asked him in passing how he was doing. Without hesitation, he said it was because he thought I was like every other officer on the staff who really didn't give a damn about how he was doing, and so why should he waste his breath and answer? I assured him that wasn't the case with me, and that when I asked him that question, it was because I was really interested in how he was doing.

We spent the next forty-five minutes or so talking about his parents and his life before the academy. We wrapped up our conversation with each of us having a clearer understanding of the other, and by the time I opened the door for him to leave, I had really begun to like him. Seeing him later became one of the highlights of my day. I remember approaching the team for a uniform inspection before we boarded our buses for the airport to head out of town for a game. This young man was standing there, comparing the shine on his shoes to the shine of our kicker's shoes, showing off that his shoes looked better. Believe me, that was a major turnaround for him.

Years later, after I retired, that young man contacted me and asked if I would write him an endorsement to change his designator (i.e. his specialty). I happily wrote that endorsement, getting the first draft back to him by the next day. Had I never confronted him and just continued disliking him, I would have missed out on a great relationship.

My association with the football team, the coaching and training staff, as well as the Naval Academy athletic staff, was the most satisfying part of my tour. From the athletic director to the equipment interns, it was a truly professional staff. In the years following my tour and still today, I reach out to them from time to time for support, and they've answered my calls every time.

What I came to appreciate most from that tour was the time I spent in the presence of young men who were going to become the best of the best when it came to leading sailors and Marines. As I know is the case of all the service academy teams, there were men from that navy football team who would later die in combat while leading from the front, and be decorated with some of our nation's highest awards for valor. If given the choice of fighting alongside a service academy football player or anyone else, I'd take the football player every time.

CHAPTER TWENTY-SIX

WHEN EXPECTED TO LEAD, LEAD

There is a place in all areas of military and corporate business for a "show me the reference" or "what does the instruction say" attitude. Certainly when it comes to knowing and adhering to the law of armed conflict, there can be no liberal interpretation of a commander's intent. Yet even then, those in charge have to make their own judgments with respect to self-defense when a situation falls outside the lines of what's in writing. I believe a significant aspect of all performance evaluations should be an assessment of our ability to accomplish the mission without having to seek guidance or approval every step of the way.

I also know that procedural compliance for operating equipment cannot be left open to interpretation. In fact, aside from the major fuel oil leak aboard *Gates,* the most catastrophic equipment casualty I saw during my career was the result of someone violating established procedures for isolating equipment.

There is a scene in *A Few Good Men* when Jack Nicholson's character is on the witness stand during a trial. During questioning, he goes off on a diatribe defending his actions because he believes the people who put him in his leadership position expected him to lead. By being given his command, he felt it was implied he was trusted to execute his duties in the manner he thought best—especially if his actions took place in a gray area. His belief was that he wouldn't have been put in that position if his superiors in the chain of command hadn't had confidence in his ability to lead without needing their regular direction or affirmation.

Although written directions and guidance provide the framework within which decisions are made, I firmly believe most were never intended to limit a leader's ability or right to make his or her own judgment about the specific circumstances surrounding a case. I understand policies that demand zero tolerance for deviations, but I also believe commanders who always default to what is written as a basis for decisions aren't really leading. They are managing. I recognize that management is part of our skill set, but when you're able to apply leadership to a decision, why wouldn't you do so?

I remember serving as flag secretary for the commander of the Surface Force, Atlantic, when the admiral received a letter from the commanding officer of an *Arleigh Burke*-class destroyer. The letter was asking for my admiral's permission to fill one of his soda machines with non-alcoholic beer. The admiral's immediate reaction was, "Why did he ask me? He should have just done it. Now I have to say no."

Much like Colonel Jessup's rant in *A Few Good Men* revealed, I also believe the people who put us in command expect us to lead. Even if it shouldn't be said, I know there are things our bosses don't want to know. I never asked my boss to make a decision for me that was my responsibility to make in an effort to cover my ass or shift the accountability for a bad outcome. I didn't worry about whether or not he was going to stand behind one of my decisions if it went against written guidance or was the wrong interpretation of a gray area.

I remember talking about leadership with an old friend when he said making everything black and white takes the challenge and the fun out of leadership. I understand why some leaders always rely on written guidance to make decisions, and in some cases it's the best—if not all—we have. As long as a decision I made was predicated on doing the best thing I could for the person involved, I didn't care what anyone else thought. In every instance when my boss questioned my decision, my explanation was accepted without issue or further discussion. I was always open and honest about what I did and why. Furthermore, I have never had a problem with explaining my actions when asked about them, so long as there was time to do so. Obviously explaining decisions during the heat of battle is a nonstarter, but I found requests for explanations during calmer moments to be great opportunities to say things I might have otherwise kept to myself.

At the risk of sounding out of touch and behind the times with respect to technology, and with what seems to be the common practice of sniping at people with whom we have issues, I have to discuss accusations. Before email, cell phones, and hotlines, if someone had an issue with a person, they addressed it head-on or lived with it. I fully understand the need for anonymity when lodging a complaint in the workplace. I also understand the need for a process to allow employees to have their legitimate concerns addressed confidentially. I get that. However, when people feel the need to spend most of their time looking for only what they perceive to be the bad in others, that's where I take exception. No matter how justified people's reasons are for doing certain things, they are going to be questioned—often by someone who has never walked in their shoes. In many cases, the questions are valid, and from the perspective of the person expressing concern or doubt, the decision simply didn't make sense and they are trying to better understand the decision.

Once while attending a warfare commander's conference with my commodore and the other commanding officers in my squadron, I received notification from my XO that the ship had received a congressional inquiry regarding my adjudication of a disciplinary case. The letter from the congressman's office included a letter from a family member of a sailor whom I had administratively separated from the navy. The letter condemned my actions and insisted I be investigated and subsequently fired as *Arleigh Burke*'s commanding officer.

During a break in the conference, I informed my commodore and one of the other commanding officers of the letter. Both advised me to simply reply that I had taken this sailor to captain's mast in accordance with the provisions of the Uniform Code of Military Justice and to leave it at that. I said I couldn't do that, because had I been the one writing that letter to my congressman, such a response would have only angered me more and made me more determined to have the target of my letter fired.

I excused myself from the afternoon lectures and went to a conference room for some privacy to call the congressman's office. I had given the sailor in question every benefit of the doubt, only taking action against him after he had lied no less than three times. I got the military liaison for the congressman's office on the phone and asked if he could arrange a conference call with the writer of the complaint, in which all of us could address the charges brought against me.

The liaison was more than happy to arrange the call, and within five minutes of initiating my call to the congressman's office, I was in a three-way call with the writer of the letter and the congressman's liaison. As soon as the writer knew I was on the line, he immediately began apologizing for his words and accusations. He went on to explain how his physical maladies had prevented his military service and how much respect he had for those in the military.

I tried my best to listen politely, but after only a short while, I interrupted him without acknowledging his apology. I let him know I was prepared to tell him some things about his family member's conduct of which I was guessing he was unaware.

When I was finished with my explanation, he said he appreciated my response and my service, and apologized again. This time around, I accepted his apology. I asked both him and the congressman's military liaison if there was anything further they needed from me to close out the complaint, and they both replied there was nothing more to do. Just like that, the issue was resolved. Had I been evasive, I'm sure the complaint would have gained traction and would have taken much longer to resolve.

∽

One of the most significant aspects of a military career is the opportunity to lead early and often. When given that opportunity, take full advantage of it. Recognize the considerable satisfaction in serving others and the true honor in subjugating your needs and wants to the care of your people. Know your craft the best you can, so you can apply the rules as appropriate, but also give equal thought to those situations that provide an opportunity to make a positive impact. Those are the decisions that are the most rewarding.

CHAPTER TWENTY-SEVEN

THE SLIPPERY SLOPE

Some clichés and adages hold meaning for me, such as "life's too short" and "beauty is in the eye of the beholder." However, I've known people, including military leaders, who live their lives as if every cliché is an imperative or absolute. Their complete belief in those truisms guides the decisions they make. It's as if living by clichés gives them the comfort of knowing that their beliefs have already been proven valid. They share a belief that, like the clichés, their decisions are based on absolutes. It's crazy that people rely on clichés as reasons not to take chances or to be bold in their actions. The greatest benefit of being in a position to make decisions is getting to make judgments based on facts and experience—not what some common saying might assert. Clichés are so overused as to be meaningless, yet trying to explain that to a person who lives by them is often futile.

A cliché I believe epitomizes cowardice is "the slippery slope." As I made my way through my career, I was frustrated by bosses who wouldn't make exceptions to their ways of thinking no matter how much sense an opposing opinion made. Those bosses were often concerned that making exceptions would start them down a slippery slope. I repeatedly argued that the slope was only slippery if they didn't have the confidence or conviction in their decisions to prevent the slide. Refusing to make an exception to a self-imposed standard simply because you don't want to have to explain your actions is pure cowardice. Relying on clichés only gives leaders an escape from facing questions regarding their decisions—especially ones leaders think they might regret. It's a way of mitigating the risk inherent in all decisions.

Similarly, administering punishment under the Uniform Code of Military Justice is a classic example of commanders going strictly by the book, and a tendency to overvalue consistency. I have witnessed commanding officers who apply a one-size-fits-all approach to their discipline. The same offense, regardless of the circumstances, merits the same punishment. No questions. No discussion. Those commanding officers do this under the shroud of fairness or consistency, lest they start down that slippery slope. A commanding officer who goes into a captain's mast knowing their decision before even hearing the defendant's side of the story shouldn't waste time holding the mast. They may as well just implement the punishment and be done with it.

I found captain's masts to be extremely unpleasant. I would review the circumstances of each case alone in my cabin beforehand. At the proceedings, after I had exchanged official greetings with the defendant, I invited everyone to stand at ease. At every commanding officer's mast I had ever attended prior to my command tour on *Arleigh Burke*, the defendant was made to stand at attention for the duration of the hearing. How does that allow the person being charged with an offense to feel comfortable enough to speak freely? They are already at a disadvantage because standing in front of the captain is intimidating—or at least it should be.

Sometimes I would ask my master at arms what my previous punishments had been for similar offenses. However, I would use that information primarily as a reference point—not because I was concerned that I'd be questioned about my fairness or consistency later. If I was ever questioned or confronted about a decision, I openly and honestly answered those concerns and explained my reasoning.

It's impossible to please everyone. People will misread even your best intentions and actions. I can't recall how many times I have talked sincerely with people for long periods of time to have them later remember only the one bit of negative, albeit constructive and truthful, criticism I offered. Good people will appreciate honesty and strive to be the best they can be because of it. Some people can never be reached.

Much more so toward the latter part of my career, people seemed to feel increasingly entitled to an explanation for virtually every decision I made—even if a decision didn't impact that person directly. Except in those occasions when there was not time to explain a decision or action, I absolutely loved it when people asked me my reasoning behind a decision. I viewed any request as a green light to address the issue in my own words, and consequently an opportunity to explain my decision enabled me to prevent misconceptions before they could take on lives of their own. I always felt comfortable in the belief that if what I had done was done with the best interest of my people in mind, I was more than willing to accept any scrutiny my decision might draw after the fact.

CHAPTER TWENTY-EIGHT

COMMON COURTESY

The Monday following my change of command was a great day. I remember hearing the quarterdeck bong me aboard, "*Arleigh Burke* arriving." Although I had no nervousness or anxiety about being ready for this giant step, hearing my presence announced with the name of such a great man made me feel woefully unworthy. By the time I reached my cabin, though, I knew Admiral Burke would expect and deserve more from the captain of his ship—so I quickly pushed the feeling to the back of my mind. I never forgot that feeling, though. I also never took for granted the special honor I was afforded.

As everyone preparing to assume the lead of any organization does, I had spent much of my time during my training pipeline formulating how I would go about putting in motion those things I considered the foundation for the ship I wanted *Arleigh Burke* to be built upon. Although I felt life owed me nothing, there were a few things I expected—even demanded. At the top of that list was common courtesy. Both professional and personal courtesies have always been natural for me. The custom of calling someone "sir" or "ma'am" was something about the military I enjoyed. As an ensign, I saluted everyone senior to me. On my first ship, I happily called a Lieutenant Junior Grade (the next pay grade higher than my own) "sir" or "ma'am" until instructed to do otherwise. However, I would wager a bet I could sit on any naval base in the United States and witness countless lapses in standard military courtesy. I simply don't understand it. Ours is an all-volunteer force, so if a person takes issue with adhering to the rules of military discipline and courtesy, they shouldn't join the military.

Courtesy extends far beyond the salute. I always disliked when the junior person in a discussion would preface a statement to a senior with the phrase, "with all due respect." In my way of thinking, that was the person's way of justifying the disrespectful words or tone about to leave their mouth. I also never approved of a higher-ranking person using a disrespectful tone while speaking with a person junior in rank. I can't imagine using such a tone with anyone whom I professed to care about.

While military regulations govern professional courtesy, naval tradition typically guides the aspects of common courtesy aboard ships. The 1-MC is the ship's general announcing system by which information is disseminated to the crew. It is the same type of circuit used in schools to pass announcements to students throughout the school. From the day I reported aboard my first ship, it made no sense to me that when summoning an officer to either report to a location on the ship or to call someone, the words "your presence is requested" or "please dial" preceded the summons. When summoning an enlisted person to do the same, such courtesies were never used. Enlisted sailors were directed—not asked or requested—to take certain actions. That always seemed rude to me, and it served no meaningful purpose.

While one of the things I always appreciated about the military lifestyle was the clear rank structure, I never quite understood the practice of extending courtesy only to officers and chief petty officers. As an ensign, I recall being instructed on how to pass the word on the 1-MC for E-6 and junior personnel. I remember being embarrassed when I would be under instruction (observing a person qualified in the watch station before being assigned that same position unsupervised) and hear the petty officer of the watch pass an essentially rude order to someone below the rank of chief petty officer. I couldn't wait to earn my qualification so I could have the word passed for Seaman Jones to *please* dial a number. The first time I did just that, a major ass-chewing from the command duty officer followed.

Did we really believe that by extending courtesy to a shipmate who simply happened to be below the pay-grade of E-7, they would become overly familiar with someone more senior or forget the rank structure? I truly didn't understand the logic behind it. In my view, it was one of those naval traditions that perhaps at one time served some reasonable purpose, but now seemed pointless. If I had been Fireman Recruit Eschbach and someone had passed the word for "Eschbach, quarterdeck," I would have walked up to the watch officer and said I was sure he had meant to put a "please" on the end of that request.

From my first day in command, the practice of extending courtesy over the 1-MC to everyone, regardless of rank, became routine. It was amazing how quickly the general mood on the ship seemed to improve. That simple policy change just made everyone feel more valued.

Never once during my command of *Arleigh Burke* did this practice of extending courtesy to my entire crew lead to people feeling that rank structure didn't mean anything. It was a straightforward gesture that didn't offend anyone, and judging from the feedback I received, it made people feel more appreciated. It helped to foster an environment where everyone, regardless of rank, was treated with respect.

∞

The final aspect of courtesy I wanted on *Arleigh Burke* was to ensure that the same courtesy we extended to one another was also shown to anyone who came to the ship as part of a civilian work force or an inspection team. Because of the complexity of the systems and equipment on board navy ships, oftentimes their repair requires assistance from civilian exerts and agencies. I had witnessed firsthand the bias some of my former shipmates had shown toward those civilians who came aboard to fix our more complicated maintenance issues. It's another one of those "which came first" arguments: was it a civilian attitude borne out of poor treatment by the military towards their presence on the ship; or was it the civilian work ethic that left the ship dirty and torn up as a result of their lack of standards in their work that caused the bias? Whatever the case, I wanted to ensure that everyone who came to *Arleigh Burke* for any reason was treated in a manner that would make them feel valued and welcome.

To that end, whenever we had a group or individual come aboard the ship for any reason, I either met them as they arrived or I stopped by at some point during their stay to say hello and thank them for being there. Consequently (I believe), we rarely had issues regarding the quality of work or the attitude of those who came aboard. Most importantly, I didn't want an experience on *Arleigh Burke* to be the reason for someone not enjoying their day. Life is too short for that.

CHAPTER TWENTY-NINE

SERVICE AND SUPPORT

By the time I assumed command of *Arleigh Burke*, I had developed a long list of things I wanted to be done my way. In addition to the courtesy and conduct, I also had some strong feelings about how leaders should support the career development of their people.

At various times during my career, I had been asked to submit to my boss input for the annual report of my accomplishments. Sometimes I had to actually write that entire report myself. I remember vividly the first time I was expected to write my own annual fitness report. Believing my boss would use my input as his starting point, and because I found it fundamentally wrong to write glowingly about myself, I turned in a very lukewarm evaluation of my performance. A few weeks later at my fitness report debrief, I was disappointed to read the report I had submitted—verbatim. The complete lack of effort my boss had put into my fitness report disappointed me greatly. I signed it, and aside from a quick thank you, I left without commenting. I guess I was thankful my boss hadn't made it worse.

The next year I was still working for the same person. I was again directed to write my own fitness report. However, this time I substituted my name with the name of an officer I admired immensely, and I wrote the report as if writing about him. When I finished writing the report, I went back and replaced his name with mine before turning in the finished report. When I went in for my fitness report debrief, the report was exactly as I had submitted it. I didn't feel any more valued by my boss, but at least I got a nice fitness report out of it.

After that experience, I vowed to never allow anyone under my command to write their own fitness report, award recommendations and citations, or provide any endorsement for a program for which they were applying. I was once talking with a friend who was a fellow commanding officer but not in my destroyer squadron. He was complaining that he had been directed to write his fitness report, and he just couldn't do it. So I told him to give me his input, and I would write the report for him.

A few weeks later, my friend went in for his debrief, and his boss—without one ounce of shame—commented that my friend had done such a nice job writing his fitness report that he (the commodore) almost believed he had written it himself.

In my mind, be it in the service or in the civilian business world, one of the major ways leaders demonstrate genuine concern and care for their people is supporting their careers with fitness reports, personal recognition, and letters of recommendation. Leaders have an obligation to evaluate their people accurately because it is the only way for promotion and selection boards to choose those most deserving of the next career milestone.

When it comes time to write a fitness report or a letter of recommendation, nothing says to people that a leader really doesn't care about them like having them write their own. The same goes for allowing fitness reports or requests for letters of recommendation to languish in an inbox for days, weeks, or even months. On the night before I detached from one of my sea duty assignments, which had been thirty-four months in length, I stood in my commanding officer's cabin with another division officer as we reviewed three years of fitness reports. That meant two of the reports were at least one year overdue. There was no debriefing and no words of thanks. Nothing. There was not even an apology from my captain for being so woefully delinquent in his obligation to provide those reports annually.

If someone asks you for a letter of recommendation to support a career aspiration, and you agree to write that letter, the person should never have to ask you about it again. In fact, unless someone is shooting at you, or you're in the middle of sea detail or some other evolution that requires your undivided attention, you should make that letter your number-one priority and finish at least the first draft that same day. Doing anything less demonstrates your indifference to your people.

Every ship on which I have ever served had something known as the "Commanding Officer's Suggestion Box." It was a means by which anyone on the ship could anonymously communicate directly with the commanding officer. Often, though, the inputs were anything but suggestions. They ranged from complaints about the hours of operation for the ship's store or barbershop to expressions of how much the writer hated the commanding officer. I've known commanding officers who have insisted the command master chief (the senior enlisted person on a ship) have a key for the box and that he or she pre-screen all the notes before the CO saw them. In my opinion if anyone was going to be seeing the notes before the commanding officer, the box should be relabeled to reflect the true recipient.

I never liked the idea of the box. I understood it, but I didn't agree with it. I knew that by being anonymous, the box was supposed to mitigate people's fear of retribution for jumping the chain of command in taking concerns directly to the CO. But in my mind, if I truly made myself approachable and had an open-door policy, why would I need the box?

My goal on *Arleigh Burke* was to create an environment where everyone pulled together for the benefit of the ship and each other. I wanted a command where people recognized that if the ship did well, everything else—including personal achievements and recognition—would naturally ensue. I told my crew right from the start that my goal was to remove the CO's suggestion box. That would indicate to me that everyone felt free to communicate ideas up the chain of command because they knew the ideas would be discussed and considered professionally.

As I thought I was getting the ship past the point where we needed the box, I received a note from one of my hull technicians who said that while he acknowledged I walked around the ship every day, no one in his division could remember me visiting them in the general workshop. I realized immediately the person was right, so I put the note in my pocket, put my ball cap on, and walked straight to the general workshop. As I walked into the space, I noticed one of my hull technicians, who also happened to be the person who had written the note, standing directly opposite me. He was facing away and toward the aft bulkhead of the ship with his arms and hands in front of his body and out of view. For a minute I didn't think anything of what he was doing. A man I had selected earlier in my tour as the command's senior enlisted sailor of the year was also in the workshop, sitting at a table barely five feet from this man, with his feet propped up as he read a paper or a magazine. As I walked farther into the room, the petty officer with his back to me and his hands in front of his body flexed his knees and then seemed to shake something. He was still pulling up his zipper when he turned around and saw me standing about ten feet behind him. The senior enlisted sailor of the year was still oblivious to my presence.

I had served in an engineering department for years, so I knew where all the drains on the ship went. I knew this kid relieving himself in the deep sink wasn't a particularly terrible thing to do from the perspective that he wasn't going to contaminate our potable water system. But seeing him use Admiral Burke's destroyer as his personal urinal set me off. After giving him a pretty good verbal thrashing, I marched straight to the bridge, got on the 1-MC, and said that if I ever caught someone else using Admiral Burke's ship as a head (urinal), I'd have that person escorted off the ship. I went on to say that from that moment on, the CO's suggestion box was being placed in layup and was never to be used again for as long as I was the captain. I very rarely acted out of anger, but I did that time. Fortunately for me, the pique ultimately served to expedite a policy that my better self had already decided upon.

I had the crew assemble on the flight deck, and I explained my thoughts on suggestion boxes and open-door policies. I wanted people to stop by and see me—more to pass on things about their lives that they wanted to share than to complain about the food. I cared about that too, but I expected the crew to try to work those things out on their own first. I wouldn't want someone going to my boss without first giving me a chance to do the right thing. I had that same respect for the leaders on *Arleigh Burke*, and I expected them to be receptive and open.

I wanted people who desired to share important things in their lives to enter my door. It could be a child's high school graduation, an acceptance to college, the birth of a child, a wedding, a death, or the results of a race—anything. I wanted to create an environment where my crew knew I cared about them and that I was genuinely interested in their lives. As it was, I was often approached about the births of children (with photographs), deaths, divorces, engagements, and virtually everything that mattered in the lives of my crew. Life on the ship was exactly as I had hoped it would be.

As for the petty officer I had walked in on as he relieved himself, I found him after I calmed down and had a nice laugh with him. He was a good kid, and embarrassing things such as that always seem to happen. The time I caught him using the ship as his personal urinal might have been the only time he decided to do that. The fact that I was there to witness it made it even more memorable.

CHAPTER THIRTY

WHAT TIME REVEALED TO ME

I said before that I wish my father had found it in himself to share with me the lessons time had revealed to him before he died. Now I'm a father of adult children, with a long career behind me, and lessons of my own to impart. I've done my best to make sure my children never feel I left things unsaid. And with this book, I hope to share time's revelations to me with a wider audience, where they can perhaps spark reflection in future generations of leaders.

On a deeply personal note, after all these years, what time finally revealed to me as I wrote this book was my mother's influence. It wasn't only all the crazy experiences I had with my father, my grandfather, or any of a number of others whose examples I followed or learned from. It was the influence of my mother's eternal optimism, her devotion and commitment to our family, and an incredible, uncanny sensitivity to appreciate in real-time those things in life that matter and make life special.

Through sadness, happiness, loss, or achievement, the wherewithal to appreciate the value of those times was something only my mother could impart to me. Unseen and unrecognized for all my years was how her quiet influence underpinned every moment I came to cherish. It was as if she had put the feeling into every experience I ever had—those incredibly special times that would have otherwise gone unnoticed and unappreciated. Looking back on how she raised me, I am amazed, given all she went through as a child, that she never once reminded me of how lucky I was to have been spared the childhood she endured. Mom was just too protective to allow us to know how bad her life had been.

I don't profess to have experienced it all or to know it all or even to have done *it* right. I only know how my upbringing's influence helped me navigate life in the navy in a manner that, although somewhat untraditional, remained true to the personal standards for which I stood. What anyone else said or thought, or what conventional wisdom may have dictated, was inconsequential to me.

Along the way, I've tried to share those things I consider absolute with those closest to me and those who have mattered most. I've already written to each of my three sons and stepsons my "what every man needs to know" speech, and for my two daughters, I've written my "how a man should treat a woman" speech. Those letters are theirs and not mine to share here. However, if I were to pass on the single most significant thing that has proven true in my life, it would be this: Life is all about the honor of your journey and how you treat those with whom you share it. Everything else finds a way of taking care of itself.

EPILOGUE

My Journal

When I assumed command of *Arleigh Burke*, my cousin Davie and his wife, Pat, came down from Pennsylvania. As I had mentioned before, Davie and I had hunted and trout fished together for years during my youth. I admired his character and courage perhaps more than anyone in my life. Although we never discussed his time in Vietnam in great detail, he did tell me on numerous occasions that his only regret from his time there was that he did not keep a journal to document his experiences and thoughts. So on the day I assumed command of *Arleigh Burke*, Davie and Pat thoughtfully handed me a journal and encouraged me to document what they knew was going to be a special time in my life.

By the time I reached the end of my tour on *Arleigh Burke*, I was on the last page of my journal. I had encouraged my crew to forward me photos of things they thought I might enjoy, and those became regular entries in my journal. One of the benefits of being the captain is that you often have time at sea to reflect on things, not just things on the ship, but things from your past. Even on those days when I spent more than eighteen hours in the pilot house, I had time to capture in words those special times and feelings, often while sitting in my chair on the bridge wing.

I kept emails that the crew sent to me, messages from the American Red Cross reporting the death of one of my best friends and other loved ones, emails that I sent home or received from my family, and my thoughts on life at sea and the sacrifices my guys made without complaint.

Even now, after almost fifteen years, I often take my journal from my bookshelf and flip through the pages. Had I never written this book, that journal would have been my children's only window into my life at sea.

Acknowledgements

I have many people to thank for their support while I worked on this book. Most significantly is my family. My wife, Susan, who believed in this effort every step of the way and was unwavering in her support, encouragement, and patience. Every word of the book was bounced off her many, many times as I constantly sought her advice. It was her outlook and perspective that kept me focused and excited about my message. I also want to thank my children and stepchildren, Matthew, Taylor, Allen, Mary, and Everett, not only for their support and advice, but for their honesty.

I also owe my friend Fran Rodgers a great deal, because it was Fran who read one of my earliest drafts and then helped guide me through the flow of the book. Fran's uncanny ability to find just the right word or the best sequence of events was priceless in tying my youth to my experience in the navy.

Captain John M. Esposito, USN, was a constant source of advice. John identified a number of key points that allowed me to more completely fill in gaps and also significantly helped tie everything together. John's friendship and encouragement have been invaluable.

Thanks also to my roommate at BUD/S, Captain Rob Monroe, USN (Ret.), and Master Sergeant Judd D. Baker, USMC (Ret.), for their support of this effort, and most especially for their friendship.

I also want to thank the following people for their review of and recommendations for the book: my cousin, Yvonne Eschbach Boyle, Mr. and Mrs. John Pohlkamp, Stefanie Joyce, Mrs. John A. Dahl,

Commander Ian Kerr, USN, Chris "Kid" Gallagher, Captain Leon F. Mahoney, USN (Ret.), Lieutenant Babatunde Akingbemi, USN-R, and Ed Fernandez Jr. Ed's advice to reorder events was critical to the final copy.

A special thank you to Linda Harber for coming up with the book's title and for her unique perspective.

Thanks to Brandylane Publishers, and specifically Robert Pruett for his belief in our message and for his kindness and friendship. Also to Tamurlaine Melby, my editor, for her willingness to understand and embrace my vision, and her genuine investment in our endeavor.

Last, I want to thank my lifelong friends and family from Southern Lancaster County, Pennsylvania, as well as the men and women with whom I served during my career for making my life's journey so special.

About the Author

Alan Eschbach was raised in the heart of the Pennsylvania Dutch countryside, where he learned the value of hard work, and developed a profound commitment to personal integrity and servant leadership. He earned his undergraduate degree from Millersville University, and holds master's degrees in national security and strategic studies, and business administration. Alan was selected as a distinguished graduate as part of Millersville University's Sesquicentennial celebration, and was the recipient of the Vice Admiral Bulkeley Leadership Award from the Surface Warfare Officer's School Command. He served on six ships, and was commanding officer of USS *Arleigh Burke* (DDG 51) and USS *San Jacinto* (CG 56).

Since retiring from the navy in 2005, Alan has worked as a senior analyst and subject matter expert, specializing in briefing navy staffs on maritime security operations.

In addition to the successes of his sailors, Alan's greatest life achievement is being loved by his five children and stepchildren, his wife, Susan, and their two pugs, Winnie and Wilma.

www.ingramcontent.com/pod-product-compliance
Lightning Source LLC
Chambersburg PA
CBHW071655090426
42738CB00009B/1537